Roselle Public Library
104 West Fourth Avenue
Roselle, NJ 07203-2057
(908) 245-5809

Reading the Bible
for
All the Wrong Reasons

Russell Pregeant

Fortress Press

Minneapolis

READING THE BIBLE FOR ALL THE WRONG REASONS

Cover design: David Carlson, Studio Gearbox
Cover image: © iStockphoto.com / eyewave
Book design: PerfecType, Nashville, TN

Library of Congress Cataloging-in-Publication Data
Pregeant, Russell.
  Reading the Bible for all the wrong reasons / Russell Pregeant.
    p. cm.
  Includes bibliographical references.
  ISBN 978-0-8006-9844-7 (alk. paper)
  1. Bible—Hermeneutics. I. Title.
  BS476.P74 2011
  220.601—dc22
                            2011015061

The paper used in this publication meets the minimum requirements of American National Standard for Information Sciences — Permanence of Paper for Printed Library Materials, ANSI Z329.48-1984.

Manufactured in the U.S.A.

15 14 13 12 11 1 2 3 4 5 6 7 8 9 10

To the Congregation of
Contoocook United Methodist Church
and to their Pastor, 2003–2011,
Rev. Sammie Maxwell

I give thanks to my God always for you because of the grace of
God that has been given you in Christ Jesus, for in every way
you have been enriched in speech and knowledge of every
kind . . . so that you are not lacking in any spiritual gift.

—Romans 1:4-5

Contents

Acknowledgments

I am especially grateful to the following members of Contoocook United Methodist Church, Contoocook, New Hampshire, who were "faithful to the end" in a seven-session Bible study based on the first draft of this book: Tom Andrew, Jane Britain, Tim Britain, Lucy Gaskell, Al Gibbs, Betsy Gibbs, Dawn Howe, Jim Howe, Don King, Katie Martel, Bruce Metzger, Dale Roberts, Fred Roberts, and Terri Stafford. I also want to thank occasional attendees Dave Buttrick, Leni Buttrick, Buck Corson, Bob Gerseny, Jim Hersey, and Jack Ward. The lively and honest discussions during these sessions gave me much help as I revised each chapter for publication and renewed my confidence that authentic Christian faith is by no means incompatible with an open and inquiring mind. Those who participated are all important threads in the fabric of a congregation devoted both to the nurture and care of one another and to strong missional outreach to a broken world that hungers for healing, justice, and peace. I am also indebted to two of my former colleagues at Curry College—John Hill and Les Muray, who share a deep concern for justice, peace, and the integrity of creation—for reading the entire manuscript and making suggestions. All, however, are hereby absolved of responsibility for any of my views with which they might disagree, as well as for the book's shortcomings.

I have dedicated the book to the entire congregation of the Contoocook church, along with the Rev. Sammie Maxwell, who served the church for eight productive years. I offer my thanks to the gracious and committed lay people for their warm embrace of me as that pastor's spouse as well as to Sammie herself. Not only was she of invaluable help in teaching the course and evaluating what I had written, but—more importantly—she is a constant source of joy and spiritual strength for me. I should also say that she knows both the importance of new beginnings and the mysterious truth that (as a recording by Peter, Paul, and Mary tells us) some songs simply must be sung as duets!

Introduction

Paying Attention to the Way We Read

Is the theory of evolution compatible with biblical faith? Are the Bible's views on same-sex relations, divorce, and the status and role of women relevant to life today? Does the Bible predict the "end of the world"? And what should we make of its statements on poverty and riches, government, and war and peace? These are questions that many contemporary Christians ask when they approach the biblical writings. But because they are also questions that interest many people beyond the bounds of biblically based faith communities, I am writing for anyone who wants to think seriously about the Bible's significance in our present-day world. These specific questions, however, are secondary to a more fundamental one, which has to do with *how* we read the Bible. Not many people who read the Bible are accustomed to asking that fundamental question, however. So although this book will address the secondary questions in some detail, I begin with the fundamental one.

"We don't interpret the Bible; we just read it."

The young woman—a student in my undergraduate course in New Testament—was adamant. She insisted that her particular religious group was not burdened by human doctrines; the members of this group relied solely upon the Bible for their beliefs. There was no sense arguing about what the Bible means in any particular instance, because it means what it says and says what it means. And, of course, this group thought of its beliefs as the absolute truth, since they were based not upon fallible human interpretation but directly upon the Bible itself.

From my perspective, however, her statement made no sense at all. My point was not so much that her reading of the Bible was wrong but that it is nonsensical to talk about understanding any sort of communication without interpreting it. It might seem that at least some sentences are so straightforward that their meanings are self-evident, so that no interpretation is needed. But is this really so? The fact is that not only the simplest statements but even individual words need interpretation. When I say the word *dog*, a hairy animal does not leap out of my mouth. Anyone who hears me use the word will have to engage in an act of interpretation to associate that word with a canine, because I might mean something entirely different. In one context, "dog" could refer to a detestable human being, while in another it could signify a wiener in a bun. And the process of making the association between this word and one or the other of these choices is an instance of interpretation.

Nor does a sentence always mean what it says. Consider the statement "That was a smart thing to do." We might understand it as a compliment that one person offers another. But we could also take it as sarcasm, meaning, in effect, "That was really *stupid*"—in which case the statement would mean not what it says but the exact opposite! And the process of discerning whether a statement is straightforward or sarcastic is another example of interpretation.

To understand any sort of communication, we have to interpret it, which means using our imagination to construe it in some particular way. And when we come to complex writings such as the Bible, the need for interpretation becomes even more evident. For example, in Mark 3:27, Jesus makes this startling statement: "But no one can enter a strong man's house and plunder his property without first tying up the strong man; then indeed the house can be plundered." By itself this statement sounds like advice on burglary. But a quick glance at the context suggests that we should understand it metaphorically.

All communication requires interpretation— especially the Bible.

In the earlier chapters in Mark, Jesus has been performing exorcisms, and in 3:22, the scribes say that he himself is possessed by an evil spirit and accuse him of casting out demons by the power of the prince of demons— that is, Satan. Jesus replies in verses 23-26 by showing that the charges are illogical: "How can Satan cast out Satan? If a kingdom is divided against itself, that kingdom cannot stand. And if a house is divided against itself, that house will not be able to stand. And if Satan has risen up against Satan and is divided, he cannot stand, but his end has come." The point is that it is nonsensical to charge Jesus with casting out demons by Satan's power, since to cast out demons is to attack Satan's own demonic kingdom. Why would Satan send one of his agents to combat his other agents? That would only divide his kingdom. So if we read the statement about binding the strong man in light of verses 23-26, we can understand the "strong man" as a metaphor for Satan and Jesus as the "burglar" who is plundering Satan's house (attacking his kingdom) by exorcising his demonic agents. *But the passage does not say this directly.* We know this only through interpretation, an act of imagination that takes us beyond the surface meanings of the words.

Perhaps nearly everyone would agree that all reading involves interpretation. But my second point may seem less self-evident. Interpretation is not a *mechanical* process. There is no magic formula for interpretation that will ensure that everyone who follows the "right" procedure will come up with the same, "right" interpretation. There are different *ways* of reading the Bible, and no one is in a position to proclaim that any one way is the only right way. This is so in part because there are many different kinds of questions we can legitimately ask of the biblical texts. We may ask historical questions, such as "When and where did this event happen?" or "Did this event *really* happen?" But we may also ignore historical questions and read the text with literary, sociological, or psychological questions in mind. These approaches are not mutually exclusive; we can ask more than one question at a time. In practice, however, it is virtually impossible not to limit what we ask. So when different people read the same text, they often understand it differently.

Beyond this, even two people asking the same questions of a text can find different answers. This may be because one person imports into the text something that is not there or assigns a meaning to a word that it cannot have. But this is not always the case. Sometimes a passage can legitimately be read in different ways. A famous example is Robert Frost's poem "Stopping by Woods on a Snowy Evening."[1] The poem depicts a scene in which the narrator stops by a wooded area to watch the snow build up. The last verse describes the dark beauty of the woods but ends with the declaration that there are promises to be kept "And miles to go before I sleep." On one level, the poem is a pleasant recitation of an experience of someone who is entranced by a scene with alluring natural beauty but decides not to linger because of the journey ahead and prior commitments. It is possible, however, to find a deeper level of meaning in it. Many interpreters understand the woods and the reference to sleep as symbols of death: there is something enticing as well as forbidding about it, but life calls us back to itself. And the interesting thing about this particular poem is that, according to my college English professor, Frost himself wavered on its meaning, sometimes denying and sometimes affirming its reference to death. Even the author could see that more than one interpretation is valid.

Sometimes a passage can legitimately be read in different ways.

This is not to say that any meaning we might assign to a writing is as valid as any other. Some readings violate what is written in the text, and some questions we can bring to a work are more appropriate to its nature than others. We could ask whether Frost's poem describes an actual event in his life, but that would probably be irrelevant to the *meaning* of the poem, as would asking where the woods were located or who the owner (alluded to in the first verse) was. To ask whether the final lines refer to life and death, however, takes us deeply into the question of one kind of meaning, just as our efforts to imagine the beauty of the scene reveals a different kind. Both these types of meaning are appropriate to the nature of a poem in a way that the other questions are not.

My final point, then, is that it is important when approaching the Bible to consider the nature of the biblical writings and to ask questions appropriate to that nature. Much of our confusion about the Bible stems from the inappropriate questions many interpreters ask of it, and the result is a phenomenon I call "Bible abuse." I mean this term in a double sense. On the one hand, it refers to the violation of the biblical writings by using them for inappropriate purposes. But the term also points to the way people sometimes use the Bible as a *tool* of abuse, a weapon to browbeat those with whom they disagree. The Bible is a collection of writings that has the potential to liberate human beings from fear, despair, and meaninglessness. It has the power to inspire them and empower them to break free from destructive patterns of personal behavior or social systems. All too often, however, it is used to oppress rather than liberate and to strike fear into the human heart rather than to banish fear. And whether the Bible liberates or oppresses us depends upon the way we choose to read it.

"Bible abuse" means using the Bible as a tool for abusing others.

A key question that will therefore be at issue throughout this book is the one Jesus posed to the lawyer in Luke 8:30 (RSV): "What is written . . . *how* do you read?" In chapters 1 and 2, I discuss the nature of the biblical writings and the kind of authority we should ascribe to them. In chapters 3 through 5, I examine various ways people use the Bible that are, in my opinion, inappropriate and even harmful. I try to show how these uses violate the nature of the texts and miss their greatest potential, but I also begin to suggest more appropriate ways of reading. Finally, in chapters 6 and 7, I describe in more detail some ways of approaching the biblical writings that unleash, rather than curtail, their power to change our lives and our world in positive ways.

Before I proceed, however, I must add a footnote to the story of the young woman in my office. Weeks after the first conversation, we spoke again, but this time the conversation was different. She told me she had left the group to which she had belonged. In abandoning that group and its teachings, however, she had not rejected the Bible. She was in a new place in her life—open, searching, but still serious about her faith. And the rigidity I had noticed before was gone. She was liberated now, free to explore both her life and the wisdom of the Scriptures in a new way. Although her group claimed that it did not interpret the Bible, members of that group had trained her very carefully in one way of reading it. Now freed from that straitjacket, she was able to reflect on *how* to read the Bible and ready to reencounter it in more exciting, adventurous, and empowering ways.

I wish the same for the readers of this book. The inspiration for its title came from an old country-and-western song, "Looking for Love in All the Wrong Places." The song describes the heartaches that come from falling in love with people who will hurt us rather than entering into mutually satisfying relationships. In a similar way, reading the Bible for the wrong reasons can be harmful rather than helpful. It can stifle, rather than enhance, what I believe is the life-giving Spirit of God within each of us; it can encourage shallow thinking rather than help us think deeper thoughts. And there is another way in which reading the Bible for the wrong reasons is like looking for love in all the wrong places. Both practices are deceptive. Persons in abusive romantic relationships often convince themselves that all is well. And many who read the Bible for the wrong reasons allow a false sense of security to mask the ways in which such reading stifles their spirits and dulls their intellects. For all such people, along with many others struggling to understand how the Bible can strengthen their spiritual lives, my hope is that they will find others ways of reading the Scriptures that will liberate, empower, and excite them.

CHAPTER 1

More than a Fortune Cookie

The Testimonies of Two Communities

How do you read the Bible? Many people read it as a source of strength in times of personal crises or more broadly as a resource for personal devotions. These are legitimate practices with which I have no quarrel. Sometimes, however, the search for help with personal problems leads people to treat the Bible as nothing more than a reservoir of personal advice: "Can you show me a passage in the Bible to convince my nephew to treat his mother better?" "Is there something in the Bible I could point out to my sister to make her stop treating me like a child?" I doubt that there are many pastors who have not been frustrated by questions like these. We can certainly appreciate the distress that gives rise to them. But the expectation that the Bible will provide specific remedies to all personal problems rests on a misunderstanding of the nature of most of the biblical writings and a lack of awareness of the grand themes that tie these writings together. Although I do not classify this "fortune cookie" approach to the Bible as a form of "Bible abuse" parallel to the approaches I will consider in chapters 3 through 5, I find it inadequate and limiting. I therefore devote this initial chapter to the nature of the biblical writings and those grand themes of biblical faith.

The Bible as Community Product

The biblical writings were collected to serve two historical communities of people. The books of the Hebrew Bible (or, as Christians name it, the Old Testament) are the products of the Jewish community, which preserved them for the community's use. The Christian church adopted the Hebrew Bible as its own and added to it a list of Christian writings that came to be known as the New Testament. Current usage of the English word *testament*, however, obscures what the word meant when first applied to the Bible. The intended meaning was "covenant," and it designated the books of the Hebrew Bible as pertaining to God's covenant with the Hebrew people and the books of the New Testament as pertaining to God's new covenant made through Christ. From a Jewish perspective, the Hebrew Bible is the book of the Jewish community,

> The biblical writings were collected to serve two communities.

and from a Christian perspective, the two testaments together constitute the church's book.

When Christians read the Bible, they therefore do so as members of a community that has continued from the first century to the present. As such, the Bible tells a story that the church feels called to tell to all humankind, the story of God's redemptive actions in human history. When any readers ignore that larger story and reduce the Bible to a personal guidebook, they miss what is most important about it.

The Story the Bible Tells

What is this story of God's redemptive actions in human history? The first five books of the Hebrew Bible, known to Jews as the Torah, recount the formation of the Israelite people set against the background of God's dealings with humankind as a whole. The plot begins, in Genesis 1–2, with God's creation of the world but quickly turns to the theme of human disobedience, or sin. It continues with a pattern of human disobedience, followed by God's attempts to repair the damage, until chapter 12, which signals God's change in strategy. Here God calls Abraham and Sarah to leave their homeland and form a new people, through whom all humankind will receive blessing. The story then proceeds through many generations of this couple's descendants, following a pattern related to the themes of covenant and promise. God has made a promise, sealed with a covenant, to make their descendants into a great people, and the plot now revolves around various crises, which threaten that promise, and God's interventions. This part of the story reaches a climax in the exodus from Egypt when Moses leads the people out of slavery and into the desert, bound for the land that God has promised them. And the Torah concludes with the people poised to enter that land.

The story continues in the books of Joshua through 2 Kings (excepting the book of Ruth). The people enter the land and conquer it, but their life there is a cycle of ups and downs. When they are faithful to God, things go well; when they are unfaithful, things go poorly. In the midst of all this, God is at work, sending messengers and intervening in various ways. And the pattern continues as the Israelites split into two nations, Israel in the north and Judah in the south.

This telling of the story ends on an ambiguous note. The sins of the kings and the people have brought disaster. The Assyrian empire has long ago destroyed northern Israel, and the Babylonian empire has now conquered Judah and taken many of the people into exile. But the final word is one of hope: the young king Jehoiachin, though in exile, is released from prison in Babylon and dines with the Babylonian monarch.

The books of Chronicles give an alternative version of the story down to the beginning of the restoration of Judah after the exile, and Ezra and Nehemiah continue the story of that restoration. The books of the prophets and other writings fill in elements of the story, and chapters 7–12 of Daniel portray in symbolic terms the history from the Babylonian exile to the second century B.C.E. But the Bible contains no further systematic telling of the Israelites' journey with God. In various ways, however, it points to a future in which God will bring final deliverance to the Israelites and redemption to the world at large.

The New Testament continues the story by proclaiming that in Jesus of Nazareth—his life, death, and resurrection—God has fulfilled the ancient promises and brought about divine-human reconciliation. It identifies Jesus with the various forms of a future deliverer envisioned in the Hebrew Bible. The Gospels tell the story of Jesus, and the book of Acts tells the story of the early church, concluding with the image of Paul imprisoned in Rome but still preaching the gospel message. The symbolism is that this message, having reached the heart of the Roman empire, is poised to penetrate the world at large. And that message is none other than the story of God's redemption of the world, with the life-death-resurrection of Jesus at its center and his expected return in glory as its conclusion.

The Purpose of the Story

This, in broad outline, is the story the Bible tells. It is the story that Paul relates, in capsule fashion, in his letters and that has been the lifeblood of the church through the centuries. It is also the means through which the church instructs each new generation and makes its witness to the world. The ultimate purpose of the call of Abraham was to bring blessing to the whole world, and the Hebrew Bible is dotted with references to God's intention to embrace all humankind. Isaiah 49:6, for example, defines the mission of an unnamed figure, the "servant," as reaching beyond Israel to bring salvation to all the nations of the world:

> [God] says,
> "It is too light a thing that you should be my servant
> > to raise up the tribes of Jacob
> > and to restore the survivors of Israel;
> I will give you as a light to the nations,
> > that my salvation may reach to the end of the earth."

In the New Testament, this sense of worldwide mission becomes more programmatic. The Great Commission in Matthew 28:19 is a classic text: "Go therefore and makes disciples of all nations, baptizing them in the name of the Father and of the Son and of the Holy Spirit." And 1 Peter 2:9 is even more explicit in defining the church's task as to tell the story of God's gracious actions in history: "But you are a chosen race, a royal priesthood, a holy nation, God's own people, in order that you may proclaim the mighty acts of [the one] who called you out of darkness into [God's] marvelous light."

The Bible contains the story the church is compelled to tell.

In summary, the role of the church is to testify to God's actions in the world, which means proclaiming what God has done to repair the broken world and restore the divine-human relationship. From a Christian perspective, the Bible is the church's book because it contains the story the church is compelled to tell.

The Story and the Rule of God

If the purpose of the story is to bring about divine-human reconciliation, we must be clear about what that means. There is a tendency in many circles of the church today to think of this reconciliation in purely individualistic terms. That is, some people are prone to think it means only convincing individuals to accept the Christian message. But this narrow emphasis on individuals is quite unbiblical. Jesus' own message focused on the coming of God's kingdom—or, better translated, God's rule or reign. The basic meaning behind the various uses of this phrase has to do with God's sovereign activity in ruling the universe and, secondarily, with the sphere that such activity establishes. The concept of God's rule is often present even when the specific term does not appear.

As we can see in Psalm 145:13, God's rule is manifest in the past, present, and future: "Your kingdom is an everlasting kingdom, and your dominion endures throughout all generations." Often, however, the fullness of God's rule seems to lie in the future. But there is considerable ambiguity as to whether that future rule is on earth or in heaven. Isaiah 11:9 points to a time when the whole *earth* will acknowledge Israel's God:

> They will not destroy on all my holy mountain;
>> for the earth will be full of the knowledge of the LORD
>> as the waters that cover the sea.

In Revelation 21:1, in contrast, God's final rule is established only with the dissolution of the present world order: "Then I saw a new heaven and a new earth; for the first heaven and the first earth had passed away, and the sea was no more."

Even in cases such as this the new order is not completely disconnected from the old. As the next verses show, we have a kind of union between earth and heaven: "And I saw the holy city, the new Jerusalem, coming down out of heaven from God, prepared as a bride adorned for husband, and I heard a loud voice from the throne saying, 'See, the home of God is among mortals'" (21:2-3b). A similar tension appears in the teachings of Jesus. The fact that he speaks of a final judgment (Matthew 25:31-46) and the resurrection of the dead (Matthew 22:23-28) might suggest that the rule of God he announces (Matthew 4:17) is a purely heavenly affair. But in the Lord's Prayer, we find a petition for God's rule to come on earth:

> Your kingdom come,
> Your will be done,
>> on earth as it is in heaven. (Matthew 6:10)

This verse employs a device used in Hebrew poetry known as synonymous parallelism: the second line repeats the thought of the first line in different words. Thus, "Your will be done, on earth as it is in heaven" means the same thing as "Your kingdom come." In other words, God already rules in heaven; the prayer asks that God's rule/kingdom now be made manifest on earth.

Whether the fullness of God's sovereign rule is conceived in earthly or heavenly terms, it always involves righting the wrongs in the world. It repairs the damage human beings have created through their sin, and the divine-human reconciliation God brings about also involves reconciliation among human beings. In short, the rule of God brings peace and justice—harmony among the various peoples of the world and a social order that ensures all share in God's gracious gifts.

God's sovereign rule always involves righting the wrongs in the world.

Isaiah therefore describes the coming golden age in terms of a harmony that recalls the perfection of Eden:

> The wolf shall live with the lamb,
>> the leopard shall lie down with the kid,
> the calf and the lion and the fatling together,
>> and a little child shall lead them. (11:6)

Similarly, Micah stresses the reconciliation among the nations of the world that allows all peoples to enjoy the bounty of the earth:

> [God] shall judge between many peoples,
>> and shall arbitrate between strong nations far away;
> they shall beat their swords into plowshares,
>> and their spears into pruning hooks;
> nation shall not lift up sword against nation,

neither shall they learn war any more;
but they shall all sit under their own vines
and under their own fig trees,
and no one shall make them afraid;
for the mouth of the Lord of hosts has spoken. (4:3-4)

God's rule is characterized by peace, and that peace is intimately connected with justice, which is defined largely in terms of addressing the lot of the poor. The following passage describes the reign of an ideal future king. The phrase "judge the poor" means to do right by them, that is, to grant them their rightful share in the blessings of God's creation.

He shall not judge by what his eyes see,
or decide by what his ears hear;
but with righteousness he shall judge the poor,
and decide with equity for the meek of the earth. (Isaiah 11:3b-4b)

The Individual and the Community

Not only is the Bible a product of communities, but the story it tells is one of community. It is the story of God's creation of Israel and the church, but in a larger sense of God's working through these two communities to create community solidarity among the peoples of the world. We should read it in awareness that its primary focus is on human collectivities—Israel, the church, and finally all humankind as God's own family.

This does not mean that the Bible has no concern for individuals. The emphasis on justice in the rule of God is a recognition that all individuals have a place in that community. Paul constantly counsels concern for the good of the community, but he knows that the good of the whole is inseparable from that of individual members. One of his main criteria for assessing whether an action is good or bad is whether it strengthens Christ's body, the church. In 1 Corinthians 14:4-5, for example, he contrasts the gift of prophecy with speaking in tongues and judges the former superior, because it serves the community: "Those who speak in a tongue build up themselves, but those who prophesy build up the church. Now I would like all of you to speak in tongues, but even more to prophesy. One who prophesies is greater than one who speaks in tongues, unless someone interprets, so that the church may be built up."

Building up the church, however, means concern for every member of it, as we see in Paul's discussion of eating food offered to idols. He knows that food dedicated to a pagan deity cannot harm a person, since such deities are not real: "Hence, as to the eating of food offered to idols, we know that 'no idol in the world really exists,' and that 'there is no God but one'" (1 Corinthians 8:4). In principle, there is no reason a Christian cannot eat such food. But Paul makes an important qualification to this principle, because not all community members will have thought the issue through so clearly: "It is not everyone, however, who has this knowledge. Since some have become so accustomed to idols until now, they must still think of the food they eat as offered to an idol; and their conscience, being weak, is defiled" (1 Corinthians 8:7). May a Christian eat food offered to an idol? Yes, Paul says, *unless* doing so would undermine the faith of a fellow member of the body of Christ (1 Corinthians 8:9-13; 10:23-30).

> Paul judged actions according to what strengthened the church.

The biblical ideal is therefore neither individualism nor collectivism but individuality within community. The Bible is concerned about individuals, but it understands individuals as parts of a larger whole. It is concerned about the community, but it understands the community as made up of individuals, each of whom is precious in God's sight.

Invitation to an Adventure

Immersion in the biblical story can be an exciting adventure. Every adventure involves some degree of danger, however, and in this chapter I have tried to show how limiting the Bible to a source of personal guidance can interfere with grasping the grand story of human redemption. Eventually, I will examine some of the more troublesome ways in which we tend to misunderstand the nature of the biblical writings. But this will involve asking some difficult questions. The larger story the Bible tells is actually made up of smaller stories. What if the smaller stories conflict with one another? Also, the Bible comes to us from the ancient world and from cultures alien to our own. In what ways might anyone suppose its prescriptions for how to live faithfully before God apply to our own time? And what does it mean when people claim to "believe the Bible," anyway? All these questions revolve around the larger questions of the ways we read the Bible, the expectations we bring to it, the nature of the biblical writings, and the kind of authority it might have for us.

CHAPTER 2

Neither Fact Book
nor Catechism

Rethinking Biblical Authority

Why Can't It Be Simple? Complications in the Story

"Why can't it just be simple?" The woman in the adult Bible class was quoting her husband, a serious student of the Bible, who had passed away a few years earlier. The lesson for this particular Sunday involved an issue on which the Bible is quite ambiguous. So with an impish smile, the woman remarked, "This is the problem my husband always had with the Bible. Why does it have to be so complicated? Why can't it just be simple?" So far, we have seen only a hint of that complexity, but it will soon be evident that the woman raised an important question. This question, however, rests on certain assumptions that we will need to examine carefully. To do that, we will have to ask about the Bible's relationship to both matters of *fact* and matters of *theology*—that is, of doctrine, or explicit beliefs.

The biblical story is riddled not only with ambiguities but also with outright inconsistencies. I note here only a few of many possible examples. According to Genesis 6:19-22, Noah took into the ark a male-female pair of every kind of living creature, with no distinction between clean and unclean animals. In 7:1-5, however, he took seven pairs of clean animals and a single pair of unclean, along with seven pairs of birds. There are, similarly, numerous discrepancies between the historical accounts in 1–2 Kings and 1–2 Chronicles. In 2 Kings 16:20, for example, we read that King Ahaz was buried in Bethlehem, but according to 2 Chronicles 28:27, he was buried in Jerusalem.

The biblical story has ambiguities and inconsistencies.

In the New Testament, Matthew, Mark, and Luke place Jesus' demonstration in the temple during the final week of his life, but in John it is one of the first things he does (2:13-22). In John, Jesus' last supper with his disciples takes place on the day before Passover (13:1); in the other Gospels, it is a Passover meal (Matthew 26:17; Mark 14:12; Luke 22:7). Also, the genealogies of Jesus found in Matthew 1:1-17 and Luke 3:23-38 disagree at many points with respect to both names and the number of generations from one point to another.

Regarding theological differences, the books of Job and Ecclesiastes stand in considerable tension with central motifs in other writings.

Job questions a notion that pervades the books of Joshua through 2 Kings and is found in a different form in Proverbs: that God rewards the good and punishes the evil in this life. Throughout the story, Job disputes that view, denying that he has brought his sufferings upon himself through sin. But Job's friends argue against him, on behalf of this "standard" theology, contending that his sufferings are indeed the result of sin. Near the end of the story, however, God confronts Job's friend Eliphaz with this blistering indictment that clearly rejects that theology: "My wrath is kindled against you and your two friends; for you have not spoken of me what is right, as my servant Job has" (Job 42:7). In Ecclesiastes, we find statements, such as 7:15, that are even more direct in dissenting from the "standard" doctrine: "In my vain life I have seen everything; there are righteous people who perish in their righteousness, and there are wicked people who prolong their life in evildoing."

The New Testament writings also contain theological inconsistencies. In Matthew 5:18, Jesus proclaims that the entire Jewish law remains in effect: "Until heaven and earth pass away, not one letter, not one stroke of a letter, will pass from the law until all is accomplished." In Mark 7:15, however, he negates the Jewish dietary regulations: "there is nothing outside a person that by going in can defile, but the things that come out are what defile." And in Romans and Galatians, Paul argues that circumcision—a key element in the law—is unnecessary for those in Christ and that for a Gentile to seek circumcision is to deny Christ. There is also a discrepancy between Paul and the book of Revelation. We have seen that in 1 Corinthians, Paul says it is permissible to eat food that has been offered to pagan deities as long as this practice does not upset another member of the community. Revelation, however, condemns the practice without qualification (2:14, 20).

The Question of Biblical Authority

What, then, do these discrepancies in both historical details and theological or doctrinal perspectives tell us? Some people think they undermine biblical authority. But this is so only if we begin with a particular understanding of the Bible's authority, which is usually expressed through the doctrines of verbal inspiration and inerrancy. According to these doctrines, God has inspired the writing of the biblical texts in exact detail, which for some proponents means that God dictated the words of the Bible. A softer version is that God has simply ensured that the Bible contains no errors of any sort. In either case, the Bible's authority depends upon absolute accuracy in both theological and historical matters. Only if this is so, according to advocates of this perspective, can we trust the Bible as a source of divine truth.

These views are widespread among Christians, and advocates in recent times have convinced many people that the church has always thought this way about the Bible. In fact, some of the earliest church leaders were well aware of the discrepancies among the various biblical writings, and many Christians through the centuries have had very different understandings of biblical authority. What I want to show now is that these doctrines of verbal inspiration and inerrancy rest upon a misunderstanding of the nature of the biblical writings, and because of this they actually encourage some people to read the Bible for all the wrong reasons.

> Inerrancy rests on a misunderstanding of biblical writings.

To believe that the Bible is divinely inspired is central to Christian doctrine. But what does this mean? The classic text on inspiration is 2 Timothy 3:16-17: "All scripture is inspired by God and is useful for teaching, for reproof, for correction, and for training in righteousness, so that everyone who belongs to God may be proficient, equipped for every good work." The first thing to note about this passage is that the Greek in verse 17 is ambiguous. It would be equally possible to read it as, "Every scripture that is inspired by God is also useful." In this case, the implication might be that only some scripture is inspired. But even if we read the sentence as "All scripture is inspired," the exact meaning of inspiration remains debatable. To assume that it means *verbal* inspiration and inerrancy is to go far beyond what the text says. We must also ask what is meant by "scripture" in this passage, and the answer is that the reference is undoubtedly to the Hebrew Bible, since the New Testament writings were not considered scripture until the second century.

In time, the church accepted both the Hebrew Bible and the writings that were collected into the New Testament as scripture, and Christians through the centuries have understood all these writings as in some sense divinely inspired. However, they have differed among themselves as to the exact meaning of inspiration and the precise nature of biblical authority. So the question is how those of us who regard the Bible as authoritative in our time can best understand these concepts.

Biblical Authority and the Biblical Story

In light of the Bible's undeniable discrepancies, some proponents of inerrancy and verbal inspiration have modified the claim to the effect that it is only in matters pertaining to salvation that the Scriptures are inerrant. But as the previous section described, the New Testament is inconsistent regarding the continuing validity of the Jewish law for Christians, and this is certainly a matter pertaining to salvation. Another fallback position is that although the biblical manuscripts that have come down to us through the centuries contain inaccuracies, the *original texts* were inerrant. But this accomplishes nothing, since anyone would still have to admit that the actual texts we have are riddled with discrepancies. And what good could the hypothetical inerrant original texts do for anyone if we do not know what they contain? The better course is to think more deeply about what kind of authority and inspiration we might attribute to the biblical writings.

One way to approach this question is to consider how and why the biblical writers went about their writing. Let us take the authors of the Gospels. The traditional view is that Matthew and John were members of Jesus' inner circle of twelve, that Mark was a companion of Paul but passed on traditions he got from Peter, and that Luke was a companion of Paul who drew upon traditions handed down by the earliest followers of Jesus. Modern scholarship, however, suggests a different understanding of how the Gospels came into being.

In the first place, we do not really know the names of the authors or who they were. The traditional titles of the Gospels occur at the headings of the ancient manuscripts, but the authors are not identified in the actual writings. The titles, moreover, are standardized—"according to Matthew," "according to Mark," and so on—which suggests that they were added only when the Gospels were brought together in a collection. Second, it appears that none of the Gospels are eyewitness accounts. Matthew, Mark, and Luke are so similar in wording that we must judge that significant copying was involved. Most scholars conclude that Matthew and Luke copied from Mark, as well as from another document, now lost, which they designate with the symbol Q. And Mark and Q are composed of small, self-contained stories that could easily stand alone if we deleted the editorial comments that link them together. So it is clear that these units of tradition were at first handed down orally. Far from eyewitness accounts, the Gospels of Matthew, Mark, and Luke were probably written late in the first century by authors who drew upon both these oral traditions and written compilations that had appeared along the way.

John, like Matthew, was supposed to have been an eyewitness account. But it is so packed with symbolism that an early church leader, Clement of Alexandria, dubbed it a "spiritual Gospel," apparently meaning that its purpose was something other than historical accuracy. Also, John 20:31 gives a clear indication of the author's intention: "But these are written so that you may come to believe that Jesus is the Messiah, the Son of God, and that through believing you may have eternal life in his name." The purpose of the writing was to bring about faith in Christ, to convey a sense of the meaning of his life, death, and resurrection, not to produce an account that was completely factual.

What is true of John is also true in some ways of the other Gospels. Despite the close similarities in wording among Matthew, Mark, and Luke, each writer modified earlier materials in order to make specific theological points. To be sure, Luke's emphasis on the twelve as those who heard what Jesus said and saw what he did seems to express an interest in accuracy. But Luke, like Matthew, felt free to edit Mark rather freely in order to make theological points.

Our attention to the Gospels has revealed some important aspects of their nature and the nature of religious tradition in general. First, tradition goes through changes as it moves from time to time and from place to place. Second, the changes are not random but reflect the purposes of those who make them. Third, those who passed on the tradition, whether in oral or written form, were not primarily interested in historical accuracy. The Gospel authors were not writing fact books, and they were not trying to chronicle events in objective fashion. They wrote *theologically*, in order to convey the religious *meaning* of the stories they passed on. More specifically, they shaped the stories they received in order to tell the larger story of God's redemption of the world. One scholar says that the Gospels are more like sermons than newspaper accounts. To use another metaphor, we might say that they are more like impression-istic paintings than photographs. And if we can accept such a characterization of the nature and purpose of the Gospels, and of the biblical writings in general, we can begin to think differently than people often do about biblical inspi-ration and authority.

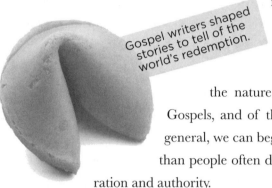

Gospel writers shaped stories to tell of the world's redemption.

Reading the Bible through a Different Lens

Those who embrace the doctrines of verbal inspiration and inerrancy expect the Bible to convey both factual accuracy and straightforward statements of theological truth. They also understand the Bible as the revelation of God in a very direct way. Although many who embrace these doctrines admit that the human authors played some role in the actual wording of the texts, they believe that God is directly responsible for the specific content of the Bible. The Bible is thus, for them, in all respects an accurate expression of the mind of God, and this means that God is, in a sense, the actual author of the biblical writings.

To persons who have never thought of the Bible in any other way, such an understanding might seem necessary if the Bible is to be accepted as authoritative for Christian faith. But this is not the only way to think about the Bible as authoritative or as the revelation of God.

To begin with, the doctrines of verbal inspiration and inerrancy are not really biblical doctrines; the Bible does not actually present itself as inerrant or infallible. As explained earlier in this chapter, 1 Timothy 3:16-17, the text that is classically presented to support inerrancy, will not bear that weight. More importantly, the Bible is not a single book but rather a library of many books, which represent many different points of view. Paul's theology differs from that of the Gospel of Matthew, and the book of Job differs from Deuteronomy. So the irony of the doctrine of inerrancy is that, despite all the emphasis it places on biblical authority, it is actually an imposition upon the Bible of a point of view that is not itself biblically grounded in any significant sense.

I cannot here review in detail the other ways of understanding biblical authority, but I will explain in general outline one broad understanding that is subject to considerable variation. It is based on a consideration of how the New Testament was formed.

Many Christian writings appeared during the first three centuries after Jesus—far more than are included in the New Testament—and were used by various church communities. To some extent, different communities valued different writings, and the process of settling upon a fixed canon (list of authoritative books) was long and difficult. Some books were still contested during the fifth century, and even as late as the Protestant Reformation in the sixteenth century, questions were raised about Hebrews and Revelation. What is important for our purposes is how the various churches and leaders made their decisions as to which books to include and which to exclude.

Authorship by an apostle was a primary criterion, and if a writing was thought to have come from the apostolic generation, it was given serious consideration also. In addition, writings were judged by measuring the content of their teaching against doctrines generally considered to be authentically Christian. As Lee Martin McDonald comments, however, "The most important criterion appears to have been church use." That is, the writings that were accepted were those that were "able to address the current religious needs and issues facing the churches."[1] Presumably, the various criteria worked together. If a writing contained teachings that varied radically from what was generally accepted as "orthodox," then it would not have been used by most churches and would not have been accepted as apostolic. In fact, Gospels attributed to various figures from the apostolic generation such as Philip, Thomas, James, Barnabas, and Mary Magdalene were rejected.

What does all this imply regarding the issue of biblical authority? It is apparent that the authority of the writings was not self-evident but was a matter of considerable reflection and debate. And if it is true that the primary criterion was use by the churches, we may conclude that the early Christian communities did not accept writings because they somehow first knew them to be authoritative. They deemed them authoritative because they found that they nurtured the life of the community. By the same token, it was apparently because they found these writings so useful that they attributed them to Jesus' apostles (Matthew and John) or other first-generation Christians (Luke and Mark). In the case of Paul's letters, we do have an apostolic author. As we will see in chapter 5, however, there is strong evidence that six of the thirteen letters that bear Paul's name in the New Testament were actually written by followers of Paul in later times.

Early Christians gave writings authority if they nurtured life.

To reiterate: the early Christian communities accepted writings into the New Testament not because they first knew them to be authoritative but because these writings nurtured church life. The problem with the doctrine of inerrancy is therefore that it reverses the process by which the church came to accept certain writings as authoritative, because it demands that we read the Bible with a prior commitment to its authority.

It is possible, however, to have an understanding of biblical authority more in keeping with the nature of the writings and the process through which the Bible came into being. Rather than imposing a doctrine of authority upon the Bible, the church should let the Scriptures speak precisely as they originally spoke—as *human* testimonies to human experiences of the divine. That is, we should understand authority as something that arises within the church's encounter with the Scriptures in its ongoing life.

What would it mean to approach the Bible without rigid, preconceived notions as to how it can speak to people today—that is, without chaining ourselves to the notion that it must yield hard-and-fast answers, either to questions of fact or to matters of doctrine? One could understand it as a dialogue partner in a continual search for truths by which to live. Given the diversity of points of view within the Bible, a community would be free to wrestle with different understandings of the faith and different answers to moral questions. Those who value the Bible would treat the Bible as an indispensable resource, but neither as a fact book nor as a catechism containing one-dimensional answers to questions of ultimate truth. To treat the Bible as a dialogue partner would mean opening ourselves to its many perspectives, prepared to have our own preconceptions challenged and overturned. Furthermore, in this kind of approach our own experiences, in a world very different from that of the biblical writers, have authority of their own. In fact, our own experiences are a necessary component in the process of negotiating the different points of view within the Bible itself.

A Christian might respond: If we take this approach, do we not give up the certainty that what we read in the Bible is God's truth? Indeed so. But those who accept inerrancy are no better off, since they cannot

Our experiences shape how we perceive differ-ent views in the Bible.

in fact *know* that the Bible is God's truth either. They can only *assume* this, from the outset, by imposing a nonbiblical doctrine upon the Bible. And one advantage of reading the Bible through the different lens I have suggested is that it honors the Bible's diversity and its origin in the human experience of the divine.

Another advantage has to do with the nature of authority. There is a kind of authority that functions coercively, imposing itself upon people as an external force. There is another kind of authority, however, that works persuasively. It convinces people "from within," treating them as active subjects and willing allies in the search for truth rather than as mere objects overwhelmed by something outside themselves.

An analogy should help here. When children are very small, they tend to believe everything their parents or teachers tell them (even if they don't always *obey* their parents or teachers), simply because in their small world these figures appear as bearers of authority. In time, however, they begin to question authority figures and demand reasons and evidence for believing something. They want to be convinced of truth rather than forced to submit to the mere assertion of truth. Good teachers or parents are able to lead children to understand *why* they should or should not accept some particular claim to truth. To understand why we should consider something true, however, we have to discover its truth for ourselves. When this happens, the parent or teacher begins to exercise a very different kind of authority. It is no longer the power to induce belief; it is rather the ability to help someone find out what to believe.

Discovering truth for ourselves involves the freedom to question what others claim to be true, for it is only through such questioning that we make truth our own. And it is just this kind of authority—the ability to help us toward belief through enabling the process of questioning—that I suggest can be ascribed to the Bible. It is in this sense that I think Christians should regard the Bible as the church's dialogue partner. In the chapters that follow, I will try to illustrate more concretely just how this process might work.

The Root Cause of Bible Abuse

"The Bible says it; I believe it; that settles it." This motto, frequently invoked in denominational squabbles, is a perfect example of a distorted understanding of biblical authority. By demanding that we first accept a particular understanding of how the Bible speaks to us, it cuts short the process through which the biblical writings might lead us to discover truth for ourselves. The Bible thus functions as a tool of abuse that stifles our capacity to search for truth and embrace it. But it also becomes a victim of abuse, because to use it in this way is to violate its very nature as a testimony of human beings to their encounters with a living and liberating God. And herein lies the tragic irony of Bible abuse: by treating the Bible as an absolute authority rather than a dialogue partner, it deprives us of the adventure of genuine engagement with the Scriptures. The Bible thus becomes an object of veneration but loses its power to speak to the human heart and bring about changes from within.

Treating the Bible as absolute authority, as a fact book and catechism that delivers unquestionable truth, is in my estimation the root cause of Bible abuse and hence the most basic among the wrong ways to read the Bible. In the following chapters, I will examine further examples of reading the Bible for the wrong reasons. But I add a reminder that my ultimate goal is to help readers find out how they can encounter these writings in ways that speak to the heart and encourage willing faith rather than rote assent.

CHAPTER 3

Neither Science nor Anti-Science

Genesis, Geology, the Big Bang, and Darwin

The young man was clearly agitated, but he continued to participate in the discussion. He was one of several teenagers gathered around the speaker after a presentation on evolution and Christian faith at a youth conference. I was pleased that the speaker did not approach the question as a matter of either/or, forcing the issue into a simple choice between acceptance or rejection of the theory of evolution. He explained several positions a Christian might take and presented each option as objectively as he could. The young man, however, insisted that it is in fact a matter of either/or. **"If anyone believes in evolution, I don't know where they're going,"** he finally said, meaning, I presume, that belief in evolution is a threat to a person's salvation. Then he turned around abruptly and left the room.

Was this teenager right? Does biblical faith demand that we reject the theory of evolution? Many Christians think so. But others have no trouble embracing it, and several denominations officially accept the notion. How we approach this question—along with the "big bang" theory and the age of the earth—depends largely upon how we read the Bible. And I believe that much of the discussion surrounding such issues is misdirected, because so many Christians read the Bible with the wrong expectations. In this chapter, I will explore both the biblical account of creation and the prevailing scientific views on the origins of the universe and human life. My goal is not to dictate that Christians must accept evolution but rather to explain why I do not believe that adherence to the Bible demands that they reject it.

A Story within a Story

We saw in chapter 1 that the creation account is a part of the larger drama of God's redemption of the world. It leads into a series of stories illustrating human disobedience, and this pattern continues until the call of Abraham and Sarah in chapter 12, which begins the long saga of God's dealings with Israel. Thus, Gerhard von Rad argues that Genesis 1 does not consider God's work in creation "for its own sake."[1] Its place in the larger story indicates that its purpose is less to explain how the physical world came into being than to give meaning to human history. In the words of Bernhard Anderson, it is a poetic creation that "intends to trace the origin and meaning of history back to the creative, sovereign will of God."[2] And Walter Brueggemann, considering Genesis 1 to have been shaped by Israel's experience during the Babylonian exile, sees it as a response of people uprooted from their homeland by a despotic foreign power. It was "an 'enactment,' done in worship, in order to resist the chaotic world of exile." Therefore, "creation is not to be understood as a theory or as an intellectual, speculative notion, but as a concrete life-or-death discipline and practice," through which God's claims "were mediated in and to Israel."[3]

If we take these scholars seriously, the real value of the biblical account of creation does not lie in any supposed factual information it might contain about the mechanics of the creation of the world. Such a judgment is consistent with what I have argued in chapter 1 against the use of the Bible as a fact book. More than this, however, needs to be said about the matter, and it will entail a consideration of the relationship between religion and science.

The Story and Modern Science

Terry Fretheim acknowledges that Genesis 1 is a confession of faith rather than a literal description of the origin of the universe. However, he questions the view that the story shows no interest in the actual mechanics of creation and goes on to observe:

> In witnessing to God's creative activity the biblical writers made use of the available knowledge of the natural world. Israel had no little interest in what we today would call "scientific" issues (see 1 Kgs 4:33). These chapters are prescientific in the sense that they predate modern science, but not in the sense of having no interest in those types of questions. "Pre-scientific" knowledge is evident in God's use of the earth and the waters in mediating creation (1:11, 20, 24), the

classification of plants into certain kinds and a comparable interest in animals, as well as the order of each day's creation. Despite claims to the contrary . . . , such texts indicate that Israel's thinkers were very interested in questions of the "how" of creation, and not just the "who" and "why."[4]

It is therefore too simplistic to claim that Genesis and modern science have no points of contact whatsoever—that, as some want to claim, they simply speak different languages and there is no overlap at all between them.[5] But if we cannot separate science and the Bible this neatly, how do we deal with the discrepancies between the scientific accounts of the origins of the universe and human beings and what the Bible says? To answer this question, we must take account of current scientific theory. But it should be helpful first to say a word about what science is.

At its base, science is simply a disciplined way of gaining knowledge through observation of the physical universe. It involves definition of problems to be investigated, the collection of data relevant to the problem, the development of hypotheses to solve the problems, and testing of the hypotheses through experimentation. Philosophers reflect on the nature of science and its methods, but science itself necessarily operates by bracketing out certain kinds of questions that belong more properly to philosophy or religion. Thus, if medical researchers want to know what causes a particular disease, they must put aside explanations that are outside the realm of observation of the physical world. They cannot, for instance, consider the argument that a particular disease is the result of God's punishment or the work of a demon. This does not mean a scientist cannot believe in God or even demons; it just means science has no means of dealing with what might lie beyond the realm of physical reality or human observation.

Therefore, when scientists ask questions about the origin of the universe or of humankind, they have to put aside religious commitments in order to let their science do its work. That is not to say that they must give up any such commitments, only that they cannot allow them to distort the process of observation. In this sense, science and religion do speak different languages, because they ask different kinds of questions. This does not mean that they have no points of contact at all, but it does mean that at some points, they must be kept separate.

Science is based on observation of the physical universe.

What, then, does the best current science say about the questions we are considering? Combining what we know from physics, geology, and biology, the scientific account of the origins of the universe and of human life goes basically like this. According to the big bang theory, the universe as we know it began more than 13 billion years ago, when an initial condition of intense heat led to an explosion and subsequent expansion that is still in progress. As the expansion continued, the temperature fell, and as it did so, there came the formation of particles, then matter, and eventually galaxies. The earth was born approximately 4.5 billion years ago, and life appeared in the form of simple cells around 3.8 billion years ago. The human species came about through a process of evolution from the simplest forms of life, through the order of primates, arriving on the scene about 200 million years ago.

But how well is this scientific story established? Different aspects of it have different degrees of certainty. The origin of the universe is the most difficult aspect to investigate, so some details of the big bang are disputed among its proponents, and some remain obscure. Some recent theorists, for example, suggest that the explosion was not the absolute beginning.[6] However, few scientists doubt the "bang" itself, and there is virtually no doubt among most of them that the universe is in fact billions of years old. The age of the earth is a much easier subject to investigate, through radiometric dating, which measures the decay of radioactive elements in rock. And biological evolution is supported by commanding evidence.

A key aspect of the evidence for evolution is the fossil record. As scientist and Christian thinker Francisco Ayala summarizes, it "shows successions of organisms through time, manifesting their transition from one form to another."[7] This, together with comparisons among living organisms and their geographic distribution, was what led Darwin to develop his theory. Today we have access to knowledge that Darwin did not, and it strengthens the case greatly. "Since Darwin's time," Ayala notes, "the evidence from these sources has become stronger and more comprehensive, while biological disciplines that have emerged recently—genetics, biochemistry, ecology, animal behavior (ethology), and especially molecular biology—have supplied powerful evidence and detailed confirmation."[8] Of particular importance is molecular biology, which allows us to identify the evolutionary history of organisms. When we make inferences from comparative anatomy regarding the evolutionary history of various species, we can confirm these inferences by studying their DNA. To quote Ayala once again, "The authority of this kind of test is overwhelming; each of the thousands of genes and thousands of proteins contained in an organism provides an independent test of that organism's evolutionary history. Many thousands of tests have been done, and not one has given evidence contrary to evolution."[9]

We may also note the astonishing variety of primate fossils that provide an incomplete but compelling picture of the evolutionary history of human beings. Evolution, moreover, can be observed in the world today. One well-known example is the way in which bacteria adapt to the onslaughts of antibiotics and return in stronger forms.

Having said all this, it is important to consider recent claims regarding evidence *against* evolution. I cannot deal adequately with these claims in a single chapter, but I will make two observations. First, it is in the very nature of science that explanations are almost always partial; theories do not have to explain *everything* to be considered verified. Second, although there is a broad consensus regarding the nature of evolution, evolutionary theorists do not agree among themselves on every detail. One of the most important objections raised by opponents of evolution has to do with the "gaps" that appear in what are claimed as evolutionary paths. As theologian Ted Peters and scientitst Martinez Hewlitt observe, however, there are evolutionists such as Stephen Jay Gould who take these gaps "as evidence that evolution has progressed by periods of no change separated by times of very rapid change. Although this does not argue that evolution did not happen, it does challenge the view that everything proceeded by a smooth, gradual pathway with the accumulation of small changes."[10] Some opponents of evolution use Gould's view to challenge the whole theory, but he is comfortable in situating his perspective under the broad umbrella of evolution. What is so well established is not some specific version of the theory but the general concept itself. And it is this broad theory regarding which Ayala can make this bold claim: "There is probably no other notion in any field of science that has been as extensively tested and as thoroughly corroborated as the evolutionary origin of living organisms."[11]

In science, explanations are almost always partial.

This scientific account of the origins of the universe and humanity differs from the biblical account not only in content but in character. Based on a systematic method rooted in observation, it is subject to verification or falsification in a way that the biblical story is not. But there are questions that the scientific story cannot answer—not because of a limitation in our current knowledge but because of the nature of science. And these are the very questions to which the Bible speaks. They have to do with what it means to be a human being and the ultimate nature of the universe itself. Does human life have a purpose? Is the universe merely physical in nature, or does it have a spiritual base? Thus, when some scientists proclaim that their theories rule out belief in God, spiritual reality, or a purpose at work in the universe, they overstep the bounds of science and enter into philosophy. A statement of the National Academy of Sciences recognizes this point: "Religions and science answer different questions about the world. Whether there is purpose to the universe or a purpose for human existence are not questions for science."[12]

Evolution is subject to verification in a way that the Bible is not.

Conversely, the biblical story is unable to answer scientific questions. Fretheim's observation that the Genesis story does show interest in questions we would consider "scientific" today serves only to emphasize that the perspective of the biblical writers was in fact prescientific and therefore unequipped to answer genuinely scientific questions. But does this mean that the biblical writers overstepped their boundaries also, confusing religious testimony with science? We must remember that the distinction between religion and science had not yet been made, and people in the ancient world naturally combined what we would call religion with a kind of pre-science without any sense of a problem. We, however, live in a very different time. When religious persons in our day ask the Bible to give definitive answers to scientific questions, they do, in my estimation, overstep the legitimate domain of religion and misuse the biblical writings. And that is particularly true when they make rejection of the theory of evolution a requirement for salvation. The apostle Paul argued that we are justified before God through our *faith*, not through the correctness of our doctrines. By "faith," he did not mean assent to theological propositions but rather a total trust in the grace of God. To condemn those who accept the theory of evolution, it seems to me, is to misread the Bible and to use it in an abusive way.

Religion and Science: Can the Two Ever Meet?

There is a sense in which we must make a sharp distinction between the kinds of questions science can investigate and the kinds of questions with which religion and philosophy can deal. But Fretheim's observation that Genesis does ask scientific questions but in a prescientific way should caution us against building too high a wall between religion and science. If we believe in a God who is creator and sustainer of the universe, it seems necessary also to believe that the various forms of truth we experience in this world have some sort of ultimate unity in God. And if so, there must be some way to integrate scientific truth and religious truth.

Some Christians try to make such an integration by attempting to show that Genesis actually coalesces with scientific knowledge. This approach is misdirected, however, precisely because Genesis is prescientific. To make this point, let us look more closely at what the biblical creation story actually says.

In Genesis 1:2, the pre-creation situation is described as a watery chaos: "The earth was a formless void and darkness covered the face of the deep, while a wind from God [or the spirit of God] swept over the face of the waters." This description parallels creation stories from Mesopotamia and other neighbors of ancient Israel, although in these traditions, the chaotic forces were understood as deities. In the Babylonian story, the god Marduk slaughters the chaos monster, Tiamat, who represents the marine waters, and creates the world out of her body. The Genesis story is obviously different, but the depiction of an initial state of chaos in a way typical of ancient cosmology should caution us against trying to correlate it with any modern account of the origin of the universe.

In verses 2-4, God creates light, but only in verses 14-18 do the heavenly bodies appear—which is unintelligible from a scientific perspective. Then, in 1:6, God creates a "dome in the midst of the waters" to create a separation within the waters and calls it "Sky." This Sky, however, is not what we mean by sky—a fact emphasized by the older translation, "firmament." It is understood as solid material, and in Genesis 7:11, we learn that it has windows, through which flow the waters that create the great flood. The action moves on through the creation of all the creatures of earth, sea, and air and, finally, human beings. Throughout the story, God performs the creative acts through the divine word alone. The process takes place in six days, and the account ends with God's rest on the seventh day. At several points, it is punctuated with God's evaluation of the created order as "good."

The seven-day sequence ends in 2:4a, but the theme of creation continues in 2:4b through the end of chapter 2. Scholars have long argued that this latter segment was originally a separate creation account. It uses a different designation for God ("LORD God" rather than "God"), and it imagines both God and the creative process rather differently. God performs creative acts not through a disembodied word but through remarkably tactile means. The male is created from the "dust of the ground" in a way suggestive of molding on a potter's wheel, and God physically breathes life into his nostrils. In addition, the process of creation proceeds in a different order, with the human beings coming first rather than last. The second story also distinguishes between the creation of the male and of the female, which contrasts with the first story. In Genesis 2:21-22, God creates Eve from Adam's rib, but in Genesis 1:27, God creates the two together.

I see no way to accommodate either of these stories to a scientific worldview. The image of the world that emerges from Genesis 1 is a bubble in the midst of waters (1:7), with a dome as ceiling and the earth itself as floor. From other passages in the Hebrew Bible, we can fill in the picture: below the surface of the earth is Sheol (Genesis 37:35), the

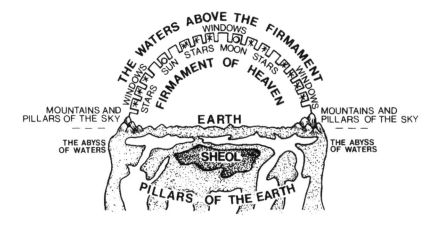

realm of the dead, which is similar to the Greek Hades; supporting the earth are "the pillars of the earth" (1 Samuel 2:8); and beyond the waters above the dome is heaven. An additional problem is that biblical chronology implies that the earth is no more than a few thousand years old—a view that some, but not all, biblical opponents of evolution continue to hold. Nor is the frequent contention that the six days of creation actually refer to lengthy cosmic epochs of any help either, since it still tries to recover a bit of scientific truth from a prescientific account.

But if we cannot correlate the biblical worldview with that of modern science, what other options are there? Few Christians today are willing to reject science altogether. Since science is based on observation, we would have to believe that God created a world in which what we can observe about the world is simply wrong. Thus, a more common approach is that of "creation science," which accepts science in principle but seeks to show that the evidence points not to evolution but to the "special creation of all things, complete and perfect in the beginning."[13] Creation scientists, however, have been unable to convince other scientists of the legitimacy of their enterprise. One reason is that their method actually inverts the scientific method. Note this clear indication that it begins with the theory of a divine creator and *then* looks for evidence to support it. As creation scientists John Whitcomb and Henry Morris state, "We take this revealed framework [the biblical account of events from creation to the great flood] as our basic datum, and then try to see how all the pertinent data can be understood in this context."[14] Science, however, does not begin an investigation with a hypothesis and then try to fit data into it. Hypotheses grow out of prior observation. In addition, scientific theories lead to new knowledge, but creation science merely looks for holes in evolution theory and then proposes its own theory as an alternative.

In fact, many Christians wary of current evolutionary theory see the flaws in creation science and embrace an alternative: the theory of intelligent design. Proponents of intelligent design do not reject evolution altogether. They argue, rather, that evolution alone cannot explain certain phenomena that, they believe, require interventions into the evolutionary process by an intelligent designer. They present their project as purely scientific and do not argue directly for the existence of God, leaving open the character of this designer. The obvious effect of their arguments, however, is to make room in the scientific enterprise for the notion of God.

In any case, a key element in much intelligent design theory is the claim that some phenomena are irreducibly complex. That is, there is no evolutionary path that could have led to them, since no part of the system could have functioned alone. Therefore they must have come into being all at once as the result of intentional design. On this point, however, the claims of intelligent design are often simply false. We do find less complex versions of systems such as the eye in existing organisms.[15] Another problem for proponents of intelligent design is that there are many aspects of existing organisms that do not seem all that well designed. Regarding the human species, we may point to the narrow birth canal of women, the blind spot in the eye, and the weak lower back—all explainable in terms of evolution.

In light of the apparent failure of creation science and intelligent design to forge an alliance between science and religion, one might think it best, after all, to keep religion and science completely separate. However, although science as such cannot pursue philosophical or theological questions, many of the theories it proposes cry out for the kinds of reflection that belong to philosophy or theology. Thus, many persons of faith who accept evolution take another approach by promoting creative interaction between religion and science. They think theology can be helpful in interpreting the results of science and that science can be helpful in thinking through religious doctrine in a way appropriate for our day. Theologians have therefore proposed various versions of evolution in which God is involved in some way other than the kind of intervention proposed by intelligent design theorists. Although science can establish the fact of evolution, it is not equipped to ask whether a divine purpose is at work in this process. As Peters and Hewlett note, however, "People of faith simply cannot conceive of the natural world without purpose or at least value"; indeed, "a purposeless creation would not be a creation at all."[16] And it is precisely the question of purpose that theologically based evolutionists address. They "affirm divine action oriented toward divine purpose in, with, and under the natural processes."[17] In chapter 6, I will discuss some implications of their views for the way we think about God and God's action in the world.

> People of faith cannot conceive of the natural world without purpose.

Reading the Stories in a Different Way

Regarding the questions with which this chapter began—whether Christians can believe in the big bang or in evolution—the short answer is this. If we do not read the Bible as science, we are free to embrace whatever truth science can uncover. And insofar as evolution and the big bang seem to be the best explanations science has at present to offer, there is no reason for Christians to reject them.

But this does not answer the question as to what value the stories can have for us today if they do not give us a literal description of how the world came into being. I therefore close with a brief indication of how a different approach to the creation story can be meaningful to us today.

We live in a world in which science and technology are so exalted that the scientific way of knowing seems to many persons to be the only way of knowing anything. Because science cannot deal with questions of value, however, it cannot tell us what is right or wrong or whether human life has some purpose beyond what we define for ourselves. Thus, if scientific truth is the only truth, we find ourselves condemned to live in a universe we view as nothing more than a grand accident and human life as part of that accident. Any values that we hold will have no grounding in anything other than our own human wills. We may, of course— as many atheists and agnostics do—assert values such as the worth of life, the dignity of all persons, peace among nations, and reverence toward the natural world. But we will have to acknowledge that these values are nothing more than human inventions and admit that they have no more grounding in the ultimate nature of things than would a contrary set of values.

If we see the Bible is unscientific, we can accept what science uncovers.

The creation story, however, offers a proposal to see life differently. It cannot prove a different view of the universe, but it does offer the opportunity to test out a different view as we live out our lives. By envisioning the universe as a work of divine creation—and as something the creator has proclaimed "good"—it makes the claim that the world we live in and the lives we live make ultimate sense. It suggests, in other words, that the universe is no accident but the manifestation of a grand purpose, of which we are a part. By naming the existing cosmic order as creation rather than chaos, it invites us to believe that the lives we live matter, not just to ourselves but to the very power that brought the world into being and sustains it. But this is not all. Because the creation story is part of the larger story of God's redemption of the world, it also invites us to believe that there is a power at work in the world, defying the forces of destruction, injustice, and oppression, to bring about ultimate well-being, or *shalom*. And, finally, it invites us to find our true identity in God, as known through a community of faith, and the meaning of our lives in serving God's redemptive purpose.

Of course, we cannot prove this vision, any more than anyone else can disprove it. Such a reading of Genesis offers neither an alternative scientific theory nor an anti-scientific perspective to be accepted on authority. It is an *interpretation* of human experience in and of the world—experience that includes but is by no means limited to aspects of reality that science can investigate. This is not to say our interpretation is a merely arbitrary set of claims that can in no way be tested. It is tested through our reason and, far more importantly, in living out our lives on the basis of the values it proposes.

The Bible claims that we live in a world that makes ultimate sense.

CHAPTER 4

Neither Crystal Ball
nor Horror Show

Understanding Biblical Prophecy

"In case of rapture, this car will be without a driver.**"** So reads a popular bumper sticker. The reference is to a doctrine popularized by media evangelists and books such as Hal Lindsey's *The Late, Great Planet Earth* and the Left Behind series by Tim LaHaye and Jerry Jenkins. Bedeviled by this doctrine, a ten-year-old boy panics when he comes home from school to find no one there. He fears that he has been "left behind" while his family members have been "raptured" to heaven.[1] And a minister in my own denomination reports her young daughter's similar anxieties. We are experiencing in our time a serious outbreak of rapture fever—enough to convince some onlookers that they want nothing to do with the Bible! But just what is "the rapture," and what is its biblical basis? I will try to answer these questions in this chapter, as I also discuss the nature of biblical prophecy and the meaning of the book of Revelation.

The Rapture Is a Ruse: How to Concoct a Doctrine and Scare Children

The belief in Jesus' eventual return to the earth is central to the New Testament, and it is associated with the coming of God's rule in its fullness. Rapture theology, however, adds a twist to this notion.[2] Prior to that final return, Jesus will come secretly to spirit away all true Christians to heaven, leaving everyone else behind on a doomed earth to suffer through seven years of tribulation before the end comes. During that period, people will have a chance to repent, but the suffering will be great, and the earth itself will ultimately be destroyed.

Where do proponents of rapture theology get the idea that Christ will return twice or that *true* Christians will be transported safely away while others, including only nominal Christians, suffer? The rapture is a doctrine that has been constructed by combining disparate passages of Scripture and forcing them into a pattern of meaning. Christians in earlier centuries knew nothing of it. It came into Christian thought through the teachings of a nineteenth-century British preacher named John Nelson Darby and became the basis of a theological perspective known as dispensationalism, gaining popularity through the *Scofield Reference Bible*. The basic idea is that God has dealt with humanity through a series of "dispensations," historical periods characterized by separate covenants. Behind this scheme is the premise that the Bible contains predictions of a future quite distant from the time of its composition.

This is a notion that many scholars challenge, and I will address it later in this chapter. For now, we turn our attention to two New Testament passages that are central to rapture theology.

In 1 Thessalonians 4:13-18, Paul addresses the Thessalonians' concerns about those in their community who have died. The issue is whether they will share in the salvation Christ brings when he returns. Paul answers in verses 15-16 that those who have died in Christ will rise when Jesus descends from heaven. "Then," Paul continues, "we who are alive, who are left, will be caught up in the clouds together with them to meet the Lord in the air; and so we will be with the Lord forever."

Christians in earlier centuries knew nothing of the rapture.

For dispensationalists, this passage means Christ will take the believers back to heaven, while others remain on earth to suffer through the tribulation. There is, however, no reason to see here anything other than a description of Christ's *final* return. Early believers, including Paul (Romans 13:11-12), expected that return very soon, and the Thessalonians had apparently not imagined that any in their community would die before that day. Their question was what happens when that end comes, and if Paul had been referring to an event *before* that, he would have had to say so.

But this is not the only problem with the dispensationalist reading. As Barbara Rossing comments, verse 16 describes Christ's descent from heaven, and "There is no reason to think that Jesus will change directions . . . to go back to heaven after Christians meet him in the air." In fact, the customs of the period suggest the opposite. Here Paul "employs a very specific Greek word for greeting a visiting dignitary in ancient times: *apantesis*, a practice by which people went outside the city to greet the dignitary and then accompanied him into their city."[3] The meaning of verse 17, then, is not that believers are "raptured" to heaven but that they go up to meet Christ in the air and then *return to earth* with him. Not only do dispensationalists read the "rapture" into the passage, they also miss the affirmation of the earth that the passage contains. The rule of God that is now brought in its fullness is apparently on earth.

In Matthew 24:37-42 and Luke 17:26-35, we have two versions of a saying of Jesus that begin with a reference to the Genesis flood as a point of comparison and end with a description of what will happen with the "coming of the Son of Man" (Matthew 24:39). The supposed reference to the rapture comes at the end: "Then two will be in the field; one will be taken and one will be left. Two women will be grinding meal together; one will be taken and one will be left" (Matthew 24:41). As the context of the passage shows, however, it describes the immediate prelude to final judgment of the world, not some event seven years prior! Matthew 24–25 is a discourse devoted explicitly to the end of the age. What Jesus says in these chapters answers the disciples' question, "Tell us, when will this be, and what will be the sign of your coming and of the end of the age?" (Matthew 24:3). And the discourse ends in 25:31-46 with an imaginative description of the judgment itself. Nowhere in these chapters is there any indication that Jesus speaks of his *preliminary* coming. Nor is the matter essentially different in Luke. Here Jesus responds to the Pharisees' question about "when the kingdom of God was coming" (17:20).

Dispensationalists cite other passages, but in all instances one has to stretch the meaning of a passage to get the desired result. In short, the rapture is a bogus doctrine with no legitimate basis in Scripture. In fact, the dispensationalists' claim that "the end is near" contradicts the

Gospel sayings in which Jesus states that no one but God knows the time of the end (Mark 13:32) and denies that God's rule will be accompanied by observable signs (Luke 17:20)![4]

Because of the distress it has caused many people, most particularly children, rapture theology must take its place as a prime example of Bible abuse. But distress to individuals is hardly its only crime. It has dire consequences on broader levels as well. For example, belief that the world is about to end and God intends to destroy it anyway is a strong disincentive for efforts to save the planet from ecological destruction.

> Rapture theology discourages efforts to save the planet.

Rapture theology also undermines efforts toward world peace. Central to dispensationalist doctrine is the notion that after the seven-year period of tribulation, Christ will return to rule from Jerusalem for a thousand years. And, according to this doctrine, Christ cannot return "until Jerusalem's Temple Mount is cleared of the Dome of the Rock and replaced with a new Jewish Temple."[5] Thus, many dispensationalists have tried to influence U.S. foreign policy in the direction of uncritical support of the state of Israel without regard to the rights of Palestinians (including Palestinian Christians). As Rossing describes the view of some proponents of rapture theology, it "is a militant all-or-nothing kind of Zionism that scripts Israel as a player in the dispensationalist Christian end-times drama in a way that baffles even Israelis."[6] War is essential to this end-times drama. Christ must win the supposed battle of Armageddon before beginning his thousand-year reign, and dispensationalists expect the end-times to be a horror show of violence and death. Thus, many actually hope for war in the Middle East, because they believe it is necessary to usher in God's rule!

The Nature of Biblical Prophecy: Reading Revelation Rightly

Dispensationalist interpretation depends largely on a reading of the book of Revelation that involves a misunderstanding not only of that book but of biblical prophecy in general. Rapture enthusiasts are hardly the only interpreters guilty of such misunderstanding, however. Many Christians through the centuries have thought that Revelation predicts events far removed from the author's time, but I hope to show that this is simply wrong.

John, the author of Revelation, names his writing a work of prophecy (1:3). But what is "prophecy"? To many people, a prophet is someone who predicts the future. The great prophets of Israel sometimes spoke of the future, but "prediction" is a poor description of what they did. They were messengers from God who announced God's intentions. They sometimes brought words of hope and other times spoke of God's impending judgment. But they were not crystal ball gazers, and they did not typically outline a future carved in stone. The message of judgment was usually also a call to repentance, so that the future remained contingent. And when prophets did point to the future, what they had in mind was usually an immediate, not a distant, future.

Also, when they spoke of judgment, they generally identified two reasons for God's displeasure: idolatry and social injustice. That is, they condemned the worship of foreign deities and the oppression of the poor by the rich. Regarding the latter theme, Amos ridiculed the extravagant ways of those "who oppress the poor, who crush the needy" (Amos 4:1) and satirized their worship as hypocritical (4:4-5). Isaiah condemned those who owned too much land (Isaiah 5:8), and Jeremiah made this blistering accusation: "Also on your skirts is found the lifeblood of the innocent poor" (Jeremiah 2:34). In a similar vein, Micah attacked Israel's rulers as those who "tear off the skin of my people, and the flesh off their bones" (Micah 3:2). To reduce prophecy to prediction is to miss the moral underpinning of the whole prophetic movement.

The book of Revelation looks to the future, but John makes it clear that this is an *immediate* future. He declares that what has been revealed to him is something that "must soon take place" and that "the time is near" (1:1-3). At three points, moreover, we read that Jesus is "coming soon" (2:16; 3:11; 22:7). Nor is this the only indication that Revelation has a short time frame in view. The book's symbolism points to realities in the author's contemporary world.

John wrote prophecy, but he did so by adopting aspects of a literary genre common during biblical times that modern scholars call "apocalyptic," a term derived from the Greek *apokalypsis*, meaning "revelation." The typical apocalyptic writer chose a figure from the distant past and wrote in that person's name. There are, for example, ancient Jewish apocalypses, written under the names of Enoch and Ezra, that are not included in our Scriptures but are available in modern collections.[7] Writing from the historical perspective of the ancient figure, the author would "predict" future events by using bizarre, symbolic language. Various beasts, for example, were typical symbols of successive empires. Then, after presenting events that had already happened as predictions, the author would write of what lay in the actual future: the end of the age. This is precisely what we find in the one full-blown apocalypse we have in the Hebrew Bible: the book of Daniel. The author, writing during the time of the Maccabean War (around 167 B.C.E.), "predicts" events leading up to the oppression of the Jews under the Seleucid kingdom and then looks forward to an immediate end of the age and the resurrection of the dead. This is all presented in symbolic language, but the references are clear to anyone who knows the history of the period.

Unlike other apocalyptic writers, John neither uses a pseudonym nor recounts past events. He does use complex symbolism to speak of future "events," however, and these concern the end of the age. But it is clear that he has realities in his contemporary world in mind. For example, much of the book concerns the fall of "Babylon," and we know that Jews of the period applied this epithet to Rome. The author also speaks of "Babylon" as the Great Whore, and the identification with Rome (the "city built on seven hills") is unmistakable in passages such as 17:9, which mentions "the seven mountains on which the woman is seated."

In addition, the designation of the Great Beast associated with the Whore by the number 666 in Revelation 13 verifies the reference to Rome. In 13:18, John invites the reader to decode the number, which suggests that it points to something the people in his time would have understood. And if we employ the method of *gematria* (well known in the ancient world), which assigns numerical value to letters of the alphabet, we find that the numerical value of Nero Caesar, according to one spelling of this name with Hebrew characters, is 666. The case is strengthened by the fact that in some manuscripts the number is 616—the value of the Greek spelling of Nero Caesar! John probably wrote after Nero's time but drew upon the legend that Nero was actually alive and in hiding and would eventually return. This does not mean he believed Nero would really return or had returned. As Eugene Boring comments, his intent was probably to say that the present emperor, probably Domitian, amounted to "Nero all over again."[8]

The book of Revelation does not give a preview of two thousand years of history. It associates the fall of Rome with the end of the age and Christ's return, but it provides no "countdown to Armageddon." In fact, although in 16:16 there is an assembling of evil agents at

Armageddon, there is no account of a battle taking place. Nor can the parts of the book that take the reader through violent and horrifying scenes be ordered into a chronological sequence leading to the end. All are imaginative ways of stating that terrible times will precede the end, and most cannot be pressed to yield literal references.

Revelation is a powerful testimony that evil will not be the final word in God's world. Scholars have named apocalyptic writings the "literature of the oppressed," and we should read Revelation as such. It is a symbolic, imaginative way of giving hope and comfort to people of faith who lived in the midst of a hostile empire. It promises the destruction of Rome and counsels believers to hold fast to their faith in the meantime; that is the point of the first three chapters composed of letters to seven churches. In making its witness against Rome, Revelation takes up the causes of earlier prophetic writings. John despises Rome for its persecution of Christians, but not for this alone. In 18:24, he indicts the empire for the blood of "all who have been slaughtered on earth." And in 18:7, 12-13, he lashes out at Rome's luxurious lifestyle and the exploitation it carried out in complicity with the "merchants of the earth," as well as for the system of slavery that supported the evil world order it maintained. This aspect of Revelation, not any supposed prediction of future events, is what links it to Israel's prophetic heritage as represented by Amos, Isaiah, Jeremiah, and Micah.

> Revelation testifies that evil will not be the final word.

Revelation 18:24 can help us find value in Revelation for our own time. Rome could hardly be held accountable for "all who have been slaughtered on earth," so it is clear that the author indicts something more than Rome itself. On one level, he speaks against Rome and the emperor he designates as 666. But on another level, his symbolism reaches beyond a specific emperor and empire. Since the number seven symbolizes perfection, 666 is also a metaphor for imperfection, or evil. And Rome stands for all imperial systems and forms of injustice and exploitation—which makes Revelation a resource of hope for oppressed people in all times and places. It is a promise that God does not stand idly by in the face of injustice but takes sides with the poor, the outcast, and the downtrodden. The tragedy of futuristic readings of the book is that, by replacing true prophecy with mere prediction, they miss this powerful witness against social injustice and undermine attempts to alleviate that injustice.

Such readings also miss something else. Despite the violent, terrifying imagery that accompanies this testimony to God's ultimate victory over evil, no passage in the entire book invites the readers to take up arms. To the contrary, as Rossing notes,[9] Revelation 12:11 describes the victory of the righteous in *nonviolent* terms, based upon the cross of Christ: "But they have conquered [Satan] by the blood of the Lamb, and by the word of their testimony." And despite the overwhelming emphasis upon God's judgment throughout most of the book, the final vision is one of reconciliation. In 22:2, John describes the tree of life in the new Jerusalem, declaring that its leaves "are for the healing of the nations." In addition, as Boring comments, in 21:24 "the very nations and even their kings . . . that had opposed God's rule and oppressed the church, are . . . pictured as redeemed citizens of the Holy City."[10]

Revelation promises that God sides with the poor and oppressed.

Second Thoughts on the "Second Coming"

The New Testament frequently mentions Christ's eventual return to earth, but it also reveals a process of reflection on and reinterpretation of this theme. The Gospel of John, for example, is notable for its de-literalization of the final judgment and the "second coming." In 3:18b-19, we find verbs in the present tense, suggesting that God's judgment takes place in the here and now: "those who do not believe are condemned already. . . . And this is the judgment, that the light has come into the world, and people loved darkness rather than light." Also, in 12:31, Jesus says, as his death approaches, "Now is the judgment of the world, now shall the ruler of this world [Satan] be cast out." In a similar way, John 17:3 defines "eternal life" as a quality of life, available in the present: "And this is eternal life, that they may know you, the only true God, and Jesus Christ whom you have sent." It is thus clear that John 14:23 refers not to a literal, realistic "second coming" but to a spiritual presence: "Those who love me will keep my word, and my Father will love them, and we will come to them and make our home with them." John also points to a resurrection "on the last day" (6:54), but the notion of Christ's spiritual presence seems to have replaced the idea of his literal return to earth.

These observations are important as contemporary readers try to work out understandings of the notions of God's judgment and God's rule appropriate to our own situation. There is much in the Bible that envisions God's rule as earthly, and the hope for peace and justice in our present world seems indispensable to the belief that God intends to redeem the world. The scientific view of the universe, however, suggests that planet earth will not last forever, no matter what human beings do: stars, after all, eventually burn out. Also, there is much in the Bible that envisions God's rule as heavenly. I therefore suggest that Christians might best interpret the hope for Christ's return in a nonliteral way—that is, as a hope for lasting peace and justice on earth. My more important point, however, is that the process of reinterpretation found in the Scriptures themselves offers an invitation to the church of today to engage in a similar process of reflection.

CHAPTER 5

Neither Rigid Rules nor Billy Club

The Nature of Biblical Ethics

The woman in the pastor's office sobbed as she told her story. This was not the first time she had consulted a minister. After suffering extreme abuse in her marriage for years, she had eventually sought advice from the pastor of her church. He had told her to stay with her husband, because the Bible demanded it. The clergywoman now hearing her story didn't know whether to be more outraged at the husband or the former pastor. And the woman sighed with relief when this pastor of another church, who read the Bible differently, took a different position. The second pastor knew what was at stake in biblical interpretation. Early in her life, she had felt a call to the ordained ministry, but there had been strong opposition to women's ordination during the time in which she had grown up. So she had delayed her dream until her late thirties, when she finally entered seminary and experienced an uplifting sense of liberation.

The fire in the bar in New Orleans' French Quarter in 1973 claimed the lives of thirty-two people. Most were members of the Metropolitan Community Church, a denomination composed largely of gay and lesbian persons; their congregation had formerly used the bar for their regular services of worship. The parents of one victim, embarrassed that their son had died in a gay bar, refused to claim his body, and several churches turned down requests for space to hold a memorial service. One Episcopal priest did hold a service, however, and after a week, a United Methodist church in the Quarter followed suit. Twenty-five years later, members of the city's religious leadership participated in a jazz service to remember the victims. They apparently read the Bible differently than did those in 1973 who would not make their space available for such an event.

Do we have, in these stories, examples of Bible abuse? If so, on whose part? Many contemporary readers find the behaviors just described deeply offensive. But Christians who hold the sort of beliefs about biblical authority that we have discussed in earlier chapters might be unsure of their response. After all, doesn't the Bible condemn same-sex relations, and doesn't the New Testament prohibit both divorce and women's ordination? Some Christians cannot understand how other Christians can justify positions that seem to violate biblical teachings. In this chapter, I will explore these questions by reflecting on the nature of biblical ethics as we examine scriptural teachings on three subjects: the status and role of women, divorce, and same-sex relationships.

How the Bible Teaches Ethics—and Why

Biblical ethics might seem to be a simple matter of divine command in which the Bible "teaches" ethics by relating God's direct pronouncements on right and wrong. Isn't that what we have in the Ten Commandments—simple, straightforward demands? Reference to divine commands is one way in which people derive ethics from the Bible, but it is not the only way. And the whole matter of biblical ethics is not as simple as it might seem.

To begin with, when we think of divine commands, we usually think of concrete rules, such as "You shall not steal" (Exodus 20:15). Sometimes, however, a commandment takes the form of a broad principle. In Deuteronomy 6:5, for example, we find "You shall love the LORD your God with all your heart, and with all your soul, and with all your might." Jesus quotes this verse in the New Testament (Matthew 22:34-40), along with Leviticus 19:18b ("you shall love your neighbor as yourself") and exalts the two commands as the heart of the Jewish law. But neither of these demands points to specific action. They are principles, not rules, and one must discern how they might be applied to concrete situations in life.

Both rules and principles are explicit means of teaching ethics, but some ethical teaching in the Bible is implicit. One form of implicit teaching is stories in which characters serve as positive or negative examples. The stories may or may not draw an explicit moral, but either way, the examples teach moral lessons. Thus, Mary's response in Luke 1:38 to the angel's message that she is to bear God's son models obedience to the divine will: "Here am I, the servant of the Lord; let it be with me according to your word."

It might seem odd to some readers to ask *why* people seek to derive ethics from the Bible. That is obviously the case for readers who do not attribute any authority to the Bible. But I also mean those Christians who understand the Bible, in one way or another, to be the "word of God," for whom it seems natural to presume that God has the right to define how God's creatures ought to live—so why even ask the question? I think most of us would agree, however, that it would be danger-ous to treat the bib-lical commandments as nothing more than arbitrary dictates, so that if we were to find a commandment to burn down the houses of anyone with blue eyes, it would somehow be "good" to do so! I therefore begin by suggesting that God's desire for human well-being, or *shalom, is a central motif of biblical thought.*

God's desire for human shalom is a central motif in the Bible.

In the story of the Garden of Eden, God provides an environment for the human beings that is clearly designed to enhance their welfare: "Out of the ground the LORD God made to grow every plant that is pleasant to the sight and is good for food" (Genesis 2:9a). And Micah 4:3b-4 is a magnificent vision of God's intention for human life:

> [T]hey shall beat their swords into plowshares,
>   and their spears into pruning hooks;
> nation shall not lift up sword against nation,
>   neither shall they learn war any more;
> but they shall sit under their own vines
>   and under their own fig trees,
> and no one shall make them afraid;
> for the mouth of the LORD of hosts has spoken.

We see in these passages primarily the outward, partly material, aspects of well-being: food, peace among nations, having a place of one's own. But other passages emphasize inward aspects. The Gospel of John promises "life" in a way that clearly indicates *quality* of life defined largely in spiritual terms. It consistently promises "eternal life," which is defined in 17:3 as the knowledge of God, and in John 10:10b, Jesus declares that he came so that people "may have life, and have it abundantly."

Ethics has to do with the good life; it asks how human beings ought to live. And if we keep in mind God's desire for human well-being, it appears that the purpose of biblical ethics is to enhance that well-being. Well-being, however, involves obligations. We may identify three types of obligations in the Bible's presentation of God's ethical commandments. First are one's obligations to God; second are obligations to one's neighbors. The third type concerns inner attitude and character, which affect one's relationships to God and neighbor but also involve obligations to self. The obligation to God is classically stated in Exodus 20:3, "You shall have no other gods before me," along with the command to love God in Deuteronomy 6:5. The obligation to one's neighbors is summarized in the command to love one's neighbor as oneself. And obligations regarding inner attitude and character are expressed in various ways, such as injunctions against anger and lust (Matthew 5:21-22, 27-30), Jesus' blessing of the pure in heart (Matthew 5:8), and Paul's counsel to be guided by the Spirit (Galatians 5:25).

It should be clear how obligations toward the neighbor relate to human well-being. Specific commandments regarding the neighbor are concerned primarily with matters pertaining to community solidarity or the common good. We can see this in the last five of the Ten Commandments, which prohibit behaviors that undermine community cohesion: murder, adultery, stealing, false witness, and coveting. Also, major parts of the Sermon on the Mount deal with matters that affect a community's ability to function for the common good: the prohibition of anger and the injunctions to non-retaliation and love of enemies (Matthew 5:21-26, 38-41, 43-48). Indeed, the Golden Rule in 7:12 can be understood in this light: when we treat others as we wish to be treated, we lay the groundwork for a cohesive group.

The obligation to love God is fleshed out by the commands regarding observances such as keeping the Sabbath, prayer, and fasting. And we can relate human obligation toward God to the theme of human well-being by noting that, according to this biblical view, human beings are fulfilled only through a proper relationship to the one who creates and sustains them. Regarding inner attitude, not only does inner *shalom* lead to outward ethical action, but it is only when our hearts are in tune with God that we truly have that *shalom*.

In summary, biblical ethics is concerned with promoting the well-being of all persons, defined in terms of our relationships to both God and neighbor and of our own inner character. It is important to keep this in mind as we approach the biblical teachings on specific moral issues.

The Status and Role of Women

We should recognize nevertheless that the social environment within which the biblical writings emerged was thoroughly patriarchal. The societies of the ancient Mediterranean world were hierarchically ordered, male-dominated systems in which persons at different social stations held differing degrees of power. The Hebrew Bible tells the story of Israel from a male perspective, and in many ways women appear as the property of men. This does not mean women were not valued, but social responsibilities were distributed largely along stereotypically gendered lines. The assumption was that all women stood in need of male supervision, and double standards prevailed in matters pertaining to sex. As Alice Laffey comments, women who engaged in illicit relations were subject to extreme punishments such as stoning (Deuteronomy 22:13-21), but there were *"no similar laws recorded which apply to either the unmarried or the married man."*[1] The Ten Commandments also reveal a male-centered perspective. There is an injunction against coveting one's neighbor's wife (Exodus 20:17) but none against coveting another's husband. And although the prohibition against adultery (20:14) applied to both genders, the offense was always understood as against a man. For a man to have sex with another man's wife was a violation of the other man's rights, and for a woman to have sex with a man other than her husband was to commit an offense against her own husband.[2]

The New Testament also reflects a predominantly male perspective. Jesus' inner circle of twelve was exclusively male, and Joanna Dewey's characterization of the Gospel of Mark could stand for much of the New Testament: "Women in Mark tend to be invisible, mentioned only when they are exceptional or required for the plot."[3] In addition, some passages explicitly consign women to subordinate status. In 1 Timothy 2:11-12, for example, we find this extreme restriction on women's roles: "Let a woman learn in silence with full submission. I permit no woman to teach or have authority over a man; she is to keep silent."

The patriarchal outlook seems so fundamental to the biblical worldview that some people are ready to dismiss the Bible completely as archaic and irrelevant; meanwhile, some Christians conclude, to the contrary, that we must accept patriarchy as part of God's revelation. However, we get a somewhat different picture of both ancient Israel and the early church if we look beyond laws and rules and ask about actual practice. The Hebrew Bible reveals notable exceptions to the subordination of women. Carol Myers gives these examples:

"Deborah is a prominent military leader who also adjudicated and is called a prophet (see Judg 4:4-5). Unnamed but no less significant are the two wise women, whose psychological acumen and sagacity play a national role (2 Sam 14:1-20; 20:14-22). Royal women, by virtue of their class, exercised political power; notable in this regard are Jezebel and Ataliah."[4]

In the New Testament, Jesus and his followers broke down traditional gender barriers significantly. In John 4:27, we find this description of the disciples' thoughts when they find Jesus talking to the Samaritan woman: "Just then the disciples came. They were astonished that he was speaking with a woman." It was considered unseemly for a teacher to converse with a woman, but here we find Jesus doing just that! In fact, throughout the Gospels, he has significant contact with women; and although there were no women among the twelve, the larger circle of disciples did include women (see, for example, Mark 15:40-41). In addition, as Elisabeth Schüssler Fiorenza argues, two Gospel passages reveal a break with the patriarchal system. In Matthew 23:9, Jesus tells his listeners to "call no one on earth your father, for you have one Father—the one in heaven." And in Mark 10:29-30, he says, "There is no one who has left house or brothers or sisters or mother or father or children or fields . . . who will not receive a hundredfold now in this age—houses, brothers, and sisters, mothers and children, and fields." The community of Jesus' followers becomes one's new family, and fathers are among the persons left behind but not among those regained in Jesus' fellowship. Schüssler Fiorenza interprets this to mean that "insofar as the new 'family' of Jesus has no room for 'fathers,' it implicitly rejects their power and status and thus claims that in the messianic community all patriarchal structures are abolished."[5]

Paul also loosens the restrictions on women. He lists many women as coworkers in the gospel (Philippians 4:2-3; Romans 16:3-5) and refers to a woman named Phoebe as a deacon and to a woman named Junia as an apostle. These latter facts are not well known, because translators have misled us. Some translations of the reference to Phoebe illegitimately render the Greek *diakonos* as deaconess, rather than deacon, in Romans 16:1. In Romans 16:7, the name Junia appears in Greek in the accusative case: Junian. But many scholars, assuming that a woman could not have been an apostle, have assumed that Junian was a shortened form of the masculine name Junianus. Because we have no evidence that Junianus was ever shortened to Junian, however, it is most likely that the text does name a woman as an apostle.

Paul did make some gender distinctions. In 1 Corinthians 11:2-16, he issues a restriction regarding women's hairstyles in worship. In that same passage, however, he makes a remarkably egalitarian statement regarding male-female relationships (11:11-12). And in Galatians 3:28, we find an even more remarkable declaration: "There is no longer Jew or Greek, there is no longer slave or free, there is no longer male and female; for all of you are one in Christ Jesus."

But if Jesus and his early followers elevated the status of women, how do we account for passages like 1 Timothy 2:11-12 that reinforce those restrictions? And how could the Paul who wrote 1 Corinthians, Romans, and Galatians also write 1 Timothy? The answer to the latter question is simple: he didn't. There is overwhelming evidence that the three writings we call the Pastoral Letters—1 and 2 Timothy and Titus—are the products of a later generation. They presuppose a later time, in which the church was becoming institutionalized, and the vocabulary is remarkably different from that of Paul's undisputed letters.[6] Terms such as "godliness" and "piety," typical of second-century Christianity, appear in the Pastorals but not in the other letters. Also, the Pastorals use the term "faith" to refer to a body of doctrine, whereas for Paul it refers to an act of self-giving. And it is significant that the severe restrictions upon women appear only in disputed letters. Ephesians and Colossians contain lists of responsibilities of persons in different stations in life, and these make gender distinctions. There is strong evidence, however, that these letters are also from a later time. They exhibit marked differences in style, vocabulary, and theological perspective from the undisputed letters.

There is one passage in the undisputed letters of Paul that restricts women's roles: 1 Corinthians 14:33b-36, which forbids women from speaking in church. However, this passage contradicts 1 Corinthians 11:2-5, which clearly indicates that women *could* prophesy in church. So there are two possible solutions to this problem. The entire passage in chapter 14 (33b-36) may have been added by a later copyist: if we delete these verses, the flow of thought is not interrupted. Or Paul may actually be quoting a point of view that he is refuting, which is precisely what he does at other points in this letter.[7]

The explanation for these discrepancies regarding women's roles lies partly in historical development. Jesus and his earliest followers broke with some aspects of the patriarchal culture and eased the restrictions on women. In time, however, the church moved from a marginal place in the larger Greco-Roman world toward integration into the dominant, patriarchal society. In the process, it lost some of its original social radicalism. So where does this leave twenty-first-century Christians faced with issues concerning gender equality?

Some Bible readers today tend to emphasize specific rules, and we find restrictive rules on the status and role of women in 1 Timothy, Colossians, and Ephesians. But Galatians 3:28 states a principle that contradicts such rules, and so does the implicit moral teaching in the practices of Jesus, Paul, and the early communities. Specific rules, moreover, are among the most culture-bound aspects of biblical teaching. All the biblical writings reflect the cultures in which they were written, but rules are less able to transcend those cultural roots than principles or other modes of teaching. Victor Furnish therefore proposes a "law of diminishing relevancy": "The *more specifically applicable* an instruction is for the situation for which it was originally formulated, the *less specifically applicable* it is to every other situation."[8] In this case, I contend that the practices of Jesus, the community, and Paul are more important for Christians today than particular rules that appear in one or another letter.

New Testament practices are more important than particular rules.

Something exciting was happening in early Christianity: traditional barriers were being dismantled, and the emancipation of women was under way. Sadly, however, it was undercut by the church's gradual accommodation to the larger culture. And so the church entered a long period in which the community found itself partly imprisoned by restrictive tradition. In our day, however, many Christians have come through experiences that have revived that early movement toward emancipation. They have seen in the secular culture how women have proved equal to men in lines of work once reserved exclusively for males, and they have seen how God has apparently blessed the ministries of women clergy. So they have learned to look beyond culture-bound rules in order to recapture the spirit at work in the early communities. What stands in the way of full emancipation, however, is the abusive use of the Bible by those who hold onto ancient, patriarchal rules and stifle the life-giving work of the Spirit.

Divorce and Remarriage

Christian opposition to divorce is based primarily on four passages in the Gospels where Jesus pronounces on the issue: Matthew 5:31-32; 19:3-9; Mark 10:2-12; Luke 16:18. All are negative regarding divorce, but there are differences among them.

In all passages except Matthew 5, Jesus proclaims that a man who divorces his wife *and marries another* commits adultery, and in Matthew 5 and Luke, he says that whoever marries a divorced woman commits adultery. It might thus appear that the objection is only to remarriage after divorce. However, in Matthew 19 and Mark, Jesus quotes passages from Genesis that trace marriage back to God's plan and then makes a statement suggesting that divorce itself is unacceptable: "Therefore what God has joined together, let no one separate" (Matthew 19:6; Mark 10:9).

In Matthew 19 and Mark, Jesus' pronouncements come in direct reply to a question from the Pharisees. In both cases, he overturns a provision for divorce in Deuteronomy 24:1 by referring to God's intention in creation, and he explains that passage as Moses' concession to the people's hardness of heart. The formula "It was also said . . . but I say unto you" in Matthew 5:31 also overturns the provision in Deuteronomy, declaring divorce unacceptable. In both Matthean passages, however, Jesus adds an exception clause: divorce of a wife is permissible in the case of unchastity (5:32; 19:9).

The Markan version ends with two distinctive elements that help explain the variations among these passages. In Mark 10:11-12, Jesus states that a man who "divorces his wife and marries another" commits adultery *against her* and then adds that "if she divorces her husband and marries another, she commits adultery." One problem here is that the Hebrew Bible does not grant women the right to divorce. And as Eugene

Boring comments, "The only instances of Jewish women divorcing their husbands are among the nobility, who live by Gentile standards and were considered scandalous exceptions."[9] The other problem is that in the Torah, adultery was considered an offense against a man but not against a woman. We thus have an example of how religious tradition changes as circumstances change. Mark's version of the saying reflects the influence of Gentile society, where women had the right to initiate divorce. We can see, then, that as the situation changed, the tradition accommodated itself to the new environment. And a similar process was at work in Matthew's "exception clause" regarding unchastity. In both instances, we see the community of faith (that is, either the Gospel writers themselves or those who passed on the sayings of Jesus before them) modifying tradition to deal with new issues.

Such a process is also evident in 1 Corinthians 7:12-16, where Paul acknowledges the right of both women and men to divorce an unbelieving spouse, although he counsels against divorce if the spouse is willing to continue in the marriage. And Jesus' overturning of a Mosaic commandment is another example of the modification of tradition. In its original form, Jesus' pronouncement probably forbade divorce altogether, but it initiated the process of further modification we have just observed.

One more variation among the New Testament passages on divorce is important. In Matthew's version of the Pharisees' question, they ask whether a man can divorce his wife "for any cause." In the background of this phrase is a debate between two schools of Pharisaic teaching over the interpretation of Deuteronomy 24:1. This verse mentions a man's prerogative to divorce his wife "because he finds something objectionable about her," and the question is what "something objectionable" means. One school said it referred only to sexual misconduct, but the other said it could be so trivial a matter as burning the husband's dinner.

Jesus takes a stricter line than both schools, but the Pharisaic debate illustrates how precarious a woman's situation was in the patriarchal system. If Jesus did forbid divorce altogether, the effect often might have been to provide protection for women.

How should Christians today view the New Testament statements on divorce? The variations in the traditions show very clearly that those who passed on these traditions modified them in light of changed circumstances. Furnish's "law of diminishing relevancy" therefore seems applicable with regard to our question. The more relevant a rule is to a specific situation, the less relevant it is to other circumstances. Jesus' pronouncement spoke to a situation very different from our own. Marriage was very different from what it is today: it was as much a contract between two families as a covenant between two individuals. Also, we can see within Scripture itself the process of wrestling with the complex issues surrounding divorce. I would therefore argue that what is required of those who take the Bible seriously today is not to choose one moment in this process and make it absolute but to join in the process and make judgments appropriate to our own situation.

> We are required to make judgments appropriate to our own situation.

The passages we have examined should remind us that Christians understand marriage to be a covenant not just between two human beings but between these persons and God. The ideal should be that marriage is a lifelong commitment, and couples should be willing to try their best to work through whatever problems they might have. But for those who believe that God desires the well-being of all persons, it is unfaithful to the spirit of the biblical witness to insist upon a rigid application of the prohibition of divorce. To perpetuate relationships that just do not work, that can bring deep psychological distress and are in some cases abusive, is inhumane and incompatible with the biblical vision of abundant life. And if we affirm the essential goodness of intimate relationships, it appears equally inhumane to deny the right of remarriage to divorced persons. In fact, what appears to be true of the ministries of women seems equally true of many marriages following divorce: from all indications, God has richly blessed them. And this is a fact that is perfectly in line with the biblical view of God as one who is always eager to offer new beginnings.

Same-Sex Relations

The Bible is not friendly toward same-sex relations. As in the case of divorce, however, we must ask why this is so. But let us first take note of what the Bible actually says on the issue.

There are only two biblical passages that explicitly prohibit same-sex intercourse: Leviticus 18:22 and 20:13. Both are addressed to males, forbidding them to "lie with a male as with a woman." Other passages are often cited in the contemporary debate over the issue, but they do not deal directly with the matter. In Genesis 19:1-25, the men of Sodom storm Lot's house in order to rape the male visitors at his home, and this contributes to God's judgment against the city. The real issues here, however, are the violation of ancient hospitality rules that demanded protection of guests and rape itself, regardless of the sex of the victims. (That is, rape of female visitors would have been equally wrong.) And it is telling that the list of Sodom's sins in Ezekiel 16:49-50 includes "pride, gluttony, excessive prosperity, and indifference to those in need,"[10] but not same-sex relations.

The creation accounts, in which God creates human beings as male and female, are often cited in debates on the issue of homosexuality, but the stories say nothing explicit in this regard. In addition, as Furnish notes, "The kinds of considerations that are usually involved when one struggles with moral issues are not present in these accounts. No consideration is given to *variations* in nature, to *exceptional* conditions, or to *particular* circumstances."[11] The assumption in these accounts is that all persons are heterosexual and capable of producing offspring. The accounts are simply descriptive and in no way prescriptive.

In the New Testament, there is nothing on the issue in the teachings of Jesus, but there are three relevant passages in the letters. In 1 Corinthians 6:9-11 and 1 Timothy 1:10, we find lists of types of sinful persons that employ a Greek word that apparently has to do with same-sex relations but whose meaning is uncertain: *arsenokoitai*. In 1 Corinthians, it is paired with another term, *malakoi*, again of uncertain meaning. The New Revised Standard Version translates the former term as "sodomites" and the latter as "male prostitutes." The rendering of *arsenokoitai* as "sodomites" is misleading, since it suggests a reference to all persons who engage in same-sex relations. The root meaning is something like "one who goes to bed with a male," but the pairing of *malakoi* and *arsenokoitai* suggests that the two terms together refer to male prostitutes and the men who use them. If this is so, the condemnation is not of all same-sex relations but of a particular type of relationship between men and boys, well-known in the Greco-Roman world, which was often highly exploitative in character. In any case, it is likely that Paul's view of same-sex relations was colored largely by his knowledge of such relationships, which were also condemned by many philosophers.

In Romans 1:18-27, Paul takes a negative view of same-sex intercourse in general, but he does not formulate a rule. He is arguing that all human beings are sinful, in order to show that God justifies human beings through faith in Christ rather than through obedience to the law (Romans 3:21-26). In chapter 1, he focuses on Gentile sin, identifying it as idolatry. Although knowledge of God was given to Gentiles in creation, "they exchanged the glory of the immortal God for images resembling a mortal human being or birds or four-footed animals, or reptiles" (1:23). After this, Paul introduces same-sex relations practiced among Gentiles as a sign of God's punishment. His point is not that God punishes Gentiles for this form of sex but that abandonment to such actions is God's punishment for idolatry. First, he makes a general statement. Because of their idolatry, "God gave them up in the lusts of their hearts to impurity, to the degrading of their bodies and themselves" (1:24). Then, in 1:26-28, he restates that point with regard to same-sex relations.

Paul's view of same-sex relations was shaped by exploitative practices.

Clearly, Paul did not approve of same-sex intercourse. We just saw, however, that his views were probably colored by his knowledge of exploitative relationships between men and boys. The other source of his views was his Jewish heritage. But what were the reasons behind the ancient Israelites' rejection of same-sex relations?

First, the Hebrew Bible condemns only male-male relations, which suggests that one concern was that they might distract men from procreation. Second, the ancient Israelites associated same-sex relations with Gentile society, and one reason for many of their laws was to distinguish themselves from Gentiles. We can see this in the fact that the law code in which the prohibitions against "lying with a male" occur is concerned largely with the "abominations" practiced by the neighboring peoples (Leviticus 18:24-30).

Perhaps most important, however, was an ancient sense of cosmic order, which the anthropologist Mary Douglas has described. Leviticus 19:19, for example, prohibits crossbreeding of cattle, wearing garments of mixed types of cloth, and planting more than one kind of seed in a field. A similar concern is evident in the distinction between clean and unclean. Animals are considered unclean if they do not conform fully to the class to which they belong. Thus, four-footed animals are supposed to walk (or hop or jump) on the earth. Insects, however, have four feet but fly and are therefore considered impure.[12]

Focusing specifically on women, Bernadette Brooten argues that this explanation "fits ancient homoeroticism perfectly." From this perspective, "Homoerotically involved women do not conform to the class of women, since they take on the active sexual roles many authors of the period describe as unnatural for women."[13] Her reference is to Greco-Roman literature, but the point holds for Leviticus as well. Within the patriarchal system, same-sex relations appear unnatural because those who engage in them do not maintain "clear gender polarity and complementarity."[14]

Where does this leave the contemporary reader? Some might argue that we must accept the ancient sense of order, since it is ingrained in the biblical witnesses. But if we do, must we not also accept the injunctions against planting two kinds of grain in the same field, wearing garments of mixed types of cloth, and restrictions on the role of women? By what right do we seize upon same-sex relations as an element of this worldview to be preserved while dispensing with other elements? We live in an environment very different from the social worlds of the Bible, as we can see in the way Paul addresses the issue in Romans 1. In verse 26, he claims that the Gentiles "exchanged natural intercourse for unnatural," clearly presupposing that same-sex attractions are a simple matter of choice. And in verses 24-26, he speaks of lust, reflecting the ancient view that those who engaged in such relations were acting out of an overabundance of sexual desire. We know today, however, that this is simply not true. There are persons who are attracted to the same sex in the same way that others are attracted to the opposite sex. Their desires are no more lustful than those of heterosexual persons, and they are as capable as anyone of forming deep, loving, caring, lasting relationships.

Paul knew nothing of such relationships, but we do. We also have a passage from Paul's own hand that can help us think about this issue: "Do not be conformed to this world, but be transformed by the renewing of your minds, so that you may discern what is the will of God—what is good and acceptable and perfect" (Romans 12:2). Here Paul lays down no rule and passes on no inherited assumptions. He urges a spiritual transformation that will facilitate the *discernment* of God's will. This implies the same kind of process we observed in the variations on Jesus' sayings on divorce in the Gospels. Discernment would be unnecessary if ethics were a simple matter of reading rules on the pages of Scripture. But it is not, as Paul well knew. I therefore suggest that we approach the issue of same-sex relations by entering into a process of discernment—one in which Christians believe the Spirit may guide us.

Many Christians in recent times have been engaged in such a process and have been led to believe, as I do, that time and circumstance have brought us to a place where we must overturn traditional views on this issue. I realize that there are also many persons of sincere biblical faith who have engaged in such a process but come to a different conclusion. Some of these have struggled mightily in their efforts to reconcile their love of their gay and lesbian friends and family members with their allegiance to the Bible. The suffering of such persons is undeniable, and I can empathize deeply with them. I therefore would hope that they could hear my testimony not as a word of judgment but as one of liberation from their agonizing dilemma. For when we learn to read the Bible differently, we no longer need to allow rules and assumptions based on ancient, patriarchal views of the world to undermine the New Testament's radical and pervasive message of total inclusiveness and love for all God's creatures.

I also believe that when we liberate ourselves from the traditional reading on this issue, we are breaking free from a form of Bible abuse, because it obscures what is deepest and best in the biblical witness and does harm to ourselves and others. And when some so-called Christians shout vicious slogans such as "God hates fags" at gay people, the abuse becomes extreme. For they are using the Bible not as a means of grace or a word of just judgment but as a billy club—a weapon to bludgeon those who are different from themselves. It is, moreover, a weapon that can kill, as anyone familiar with the suicide rate among gay teenagers knows. But a different reading of the Bible opens another way for us. When Jesus told the parable of the Good Samaritan (Luke 10:25-37), he made an unexpected person—someone the people of Judea and Galilee considered their enemy—into the hero of the story. He thus tore down a wall of separation and expanded the meaning of "neighbor." I believe it is long past time for heterosexual Christians to embrace their lesbian and gay neighbors, not as sinful or damaged people to be converted or healed (any more than is anyone else) but as sisters and brothers to be loved, accepted, and affirmed as they are.

If we do this, it becomes difficult to accept the restrictions (such as denial of marriage rights) that some people want to place on the relationships of their sisters and brothers, even as they claim to accept them on one level. Indeed, judging from the quality of many same-sex relationships, we have as much reason to believe God has blessed these unions as we do that God has blessed the ministries of women and marriages after divorce.

CHAPTER 6

The Bible and Our Beliefs

Reflections on Christian Doctrine

So far, I have focused on what I consider misuses of the Bible, although I have tried to indicate some better approaches. In this chapter and the next, I will continue to identify ways of reading the Bible that I find inadequate, but my major concern will be to show how the Bible can help Christians in particular think through their beliefs and faithful patterns of moral action.

God, Power, Evil, and Evolution

When I was in high school, two teenage boys I knew were fishing from a bridge when one had a seizure and fell into the water. His friend dived in and tried to save him, but could not. The parents of the drowned boy were devastated, but they took comfort in their belief that in some way, beyond human understanding, their loss was part of God's plan. Something in me, however, recoiled at the notion that this stark tragedy was God's doing. I could not believe that God would intentionally cut a life so short and bring such agony to a family. Nor could I find comfort in such an explanation in later years when my brother died of a brain tumor, or when Hurricane Katrina devastated New Orleans and the Gulf Coast, or when an earthquake caused unimaginable suffering in Haiti.

The Power of God in Classical Theology

Theologians have long puzzled over "the problem of evil"—the question of why a good God would allow tragic things to happen in the world. It is a serious problem, probably the most frequent reason for a loss of faith by both Christians and Jews. And it is rooted partly in the way theologians have thought about God. Therefore, I begin with a brief discussion of the classical Christian understanding of God. What I am describing, however, is not necessarily the way "ordinary" Christians have thought but the ideas of the great theologians who shaped the doctrines of the church.

The God of classical theology is all-powerful and unchanging. Both these notions are related to the understanding of God as Perfect Being. To be perfect, on this understanding, is to be lacking in nothing. Therefore, God must in no way be deficient in power. Nor can God change, since to change would imply a deficiency needing to be filled. For some classical theologians, the emphasis on God's all-powerful nature, or omnipotence, meant that God must be in full control of everything that happens in the world. So one school of thought has embraced the notion of divine predestination: God preordains those who will be saved and those who will not. Other thinkers have disagreed, stressing human free will, while yet others have embraced both notions in paradoxical formulations. But there has always been some tension between the notion of human free will and God's omnipotence.

Less familiar to "ordinary" Christians are the issues that arise when we combine the notion that God does not change with belief in God's love. The question is how God can love without being changed, since love changes us profoundly. On this point, popular Christian thought tends to deviate from classical theology: most Christians think of God as deeply affected by relationships with people in the world. But the problem remains: How, then, can God be unchanging?

The most difficult problem with traditional theology is the problem of evil. If God is both all-powerful and perfectly good, why is there so much evil in the world? Those who stress human free will can give a partial answer by arguing that free will is necessary for life to be meaningful. God cannot banish all evil without destroying the human capacity for choice. Thus, the argument goes, God could banish all evil but chooses not to, in order to allow free will. This answer, however, ignores the problem of *natural* evil—the suffering caused by earthquakes, diseases, accidents, and the like. Why does God allow (or send!) such suffering?

It is important, in exploring these issues, to ask about the sources of classical theology. Where did those who shaped traditional Christian theology get their ideas? To some extent, these ideas come from the

> Most Christians think of God as deeply affected by people in the world.

Bible. The notion of God's power, for example, is everywhere evident in Scripture, and some passages imply omnipotence. In Matthew 19:26, Jesus says that "for God all things are possible," and in the Hebrew Bible, Job addresses God with this expression of faith: "I know that you can do all things, and that no purpose of yours can be thwarted" (Job 42:2). Other passages suggest not only that God *can* do all things, but that God actually *does* all things—that is, controls everything in the world. In Exodus 10:27, we read that it is God who causes Pharaoh to refuse to let the Hebrew people go: "The LORD hardened Pharaoh's heart, and he was unwilling to let them go." God is thus portrayed as using Pharaoh as a tool for manifesting divine power (10:1). The idea that God is unchanging also has biblical support. James 1:17 characterizes God as "the Father of lights, with whom there is no variation or shadow due to change."

The Bible, however, is only one of two major sources for traditional theology; the other is ancient Greek philosophy. Plato thought things that change are less "real" than things that do not. He sought to identify what is most stable in the universe amid all the things that are affected by time and circumstance, and he found this in what he called the eternal "forms" or "ideas." More real than an actual chair, for example, is the *idea* of a chair, and more real than the imperfect justice of any society is the *idea* of perfect justice. These remain the same forever. Formal Christian doctrine began to take shape in a world dominated by this kind of thinking. Thus, as early Christian thinkers began to formulate their doctrines in a systematic way, they made use of Greek ideas. Consequently, much of what I noted regarding God's power and unchanging character is rooted less in biblical thought than in Greek philosophy. We can see this as we take note of some contrary ways of thinking in the Bible.

Countercurrents in Biblical Thought

Numerous passages of the Bible suggest that God does *not* control all things. For example, a strain of thought in Exodus contradicts the notion that God hardened Pharaoh's heart. In 9:34, Pharaoh's decision lies squarely on his own shoulders: "But when Pharaoh saw that the rain and the hail and the thunder had ceased, he sinned once more and hardened his heart." Although the Bible sometimes implies that God controls human decisions, it more consistently holds human beings responsible for their own deeds. Similarly, despite the Bible's assurances that God's purposes cannot ultimately be thwarted, it leaves much room for contingency in the world of human events. In many cases, God acts through agents in the world, so that the outcome is dependent on their cooperation. Moses and Jeremiah resist God's call (Exodus 3:11, 13; Jeremiah 1:6). The messages of the prophets, John the Baptist, and Jesus are filled with calls to repentance, which make no sense if God controls human response. And although the Bible often depicts God's actions as coercive, God acts differently through Jesus. It is not through force but through love and self-sacrifice—as seen in the cross of Christ—that God redeems the world.

Nor does the Bible consistently present God as unchanging. The Hebrew Bible is filled with accounts of God's experience of anger or pleasure, and in many instances, God changes God's mind. In Genesis 18:22-33, Abraham succeeds in bargaining with God over the number of righteous people in Sodom needed to dissuade God from destroying the city. And Hosea records God's internal debate as to how to deal with recalcitrant Israel: "My heart recoils within me; my compassion grows warm and tender. I will not execute my fierce anger; I will not again destroy Ephraim" (Hosea 11:8c-9a).

Modern Science, the Universe, and the Power of God

Much traditional thinking about God has resulted from favoring some strains of biblical thought over others and from the use of Greek philosophy to interpret those strains. But other strains of biblical thought are more in keeping with our modern experience, and the Greek emphasis upon what is unchanging does not fit well with how we view the world today. Science has brought a new understanding of the nature of the universe. We once thought of it as essentially stable, so that whatever changes might take place are mere variations on preexistent patterns. Recent science, however, reveals a dynamic universe. It is not only expanding but ever-changing. The appearance of particles, then galaxies, then life, then a stunning array of life forms—all these developments are part of a process of constant change.

We are also learning that all things in the universe are interrelated: the loss of one, seemingly insignificant life form has wide-ranging effects upon the entire ecosystem. We live, in fact, within a dynamic *system* in which nothing exists unto itself. And some philosophers argue that nothing is what it is in and of itself. It might seem, for example, that a child is a totally separate being from a parent—until we consider that the parents' DNA has been replicated in the child! And I cannot think of myself except as someone who has been influenced by my parents, my wife, my siblings, my teachers, my friends, the church, the places I have lived, and innumerable specific experiences. I am not just a person to whom certain things have happened; I am who I am *because of* these experiences. In a real sense, I am

> We live in a universe that is not only dynamic, but relational.

made up of them. We live in a universe that is not only dynamic but relational. To be at all is to be in relation.

But if God's universe is ever-changing, why should we try to make God an exception to this aspect of reality? Why not, rather, think of God as the primary exemplification of it? Traditional theology stresses that God's perfection means that nothing can or need be added to God. But to be in relation is to have new experiences, and to love is to undergo change. Why not, then, think of God as perfect in relatedness, capable of perfect love and the perfect integration of new experiences, whose changing feelings represent the perfect evaluation of any situation?

If we understand God in this way, we will think differently about God's power. Some theologians distinguish between two types of power: coercive power and persuasive power. Coercive power is unilateral; it forces from without. Persuasive power works from within, just like the kind of authority I mentioned in chapter 1. It is relational power, because it works not by itself but in relation to other powers. That is, it is qualified by the presence of other powers and is not all-consuming. To be, after all, is to have some degree of power. If either God or the forces of nature or society make all my decisions, I do not exist at all in any meaningful sense.

To think of God's power as persuasive, or relational, would help immensely with the problem of evil, for we would not have to hold God responsible for the evil in the world. And this applies not only to the evil human beings do but to the harm done by natural forces. God does not control my decisions, and they would be meaningless if God did. But neither, from this perspective, does God totally control the forces of nature. Modern physics has discovered a degree of chance or indeterminacy at the very smallest levels of matter. And just as we can understand human free will as a more highly evolved instance of such "freedom," we can understand natural forces similarly. A seizure that causes a young person to fall off a bridge and drown is a tragic accident, not an "act of God."

God and Evolution Revisited

In chapter 3, I noted that many theologians have proposed theories of evolution that make room for belief in God. Some argue that God starts the process and lets it proceed on its own, but I think the understanding of God's power I just described suggests a better option. If we understand God's power as persuasive, we can think of God as working in and through the evolutionary process—the evolution of the universe itself as well as the human species. God neither forces the outcome of the process nor abandons it to mere chance but works persuasively, in relation to natural forces, toward ever more complex forms of life. God seeks complexity, which increases the richness of experience, and complexity leads to consciousness and eventually to creatures capable of love and moral action. Why do some organisms, including ourselves, seem imperfectly designed? Because they were not in fact "designed" on a drawing board but were coaxed into being by a relational God wielding persuasive power. But why is there such a process at all, and why has it resulted in the appearance of creatures capable of love and moral action? Because God, too, is relational and lures the evolutionary process so that creatures may have ever deeper relationships, both among themselves and with God.

We can think of God working persuasively through evolution.

In proposing this way of thinking about God's power, I have obviously gone beyond what the Bible says. But so does traditional theology and any theology that tries to state Christian doctrine in a systematic way. For, as we have seen, the Bible is riddled with inconsistencies. Any attempt to make logical sense of them involves us not only in a process of selection but also in dialogue with wisdom drawn from human experience generally. Classical theology drew upon the thought world in which it was born, and theologians today draw upon the knowledge and experience unique to our time.

This does not mean we leave the Bible aside. The vision I propose draws heavily upon scriptural themes, and primary among these is God's love: God chooses Israel out of love (Deuteronomy 7:7-8); God loves those who are in Christ (John 16:27); God loves the world (John 3:16); and God loves those who are in sin (Romans 5:8). Indeed, love is so central to God's being that the author of 1 John can say that "God is love" (1 John 4:8, 16). I would also argue that it is out of love that God uses persuasive power to give purpose to the evolutionary process. And the persuasive power of God's love is evident in what God does to redeem a corrupted world. As Paul writes in Romans 5:8, "But God proves his love for us in that while we were still sinners Christ died for us." This notion—that the cross of Christ brings about human salvation—is the subject of the section that follows.

Christ, the Cross, and the New Creation

"What about Socrates?" I asked. "He's in hell today," my coworker answered. We were seminary students, from different schools, who worked part-time at a YMCA. I asked next about Mahatma Gandhi and got the same answer: he, too, along with everyone else outside of Christ, is utterly lost. Such is the view of Christian exclusivism: only those who explicitly embrace Christ can be saved. This doctrine is usually supported by two passages in the New Testament, John 14:6 and Acts 4:12. But do these passages really make such a declaration? And is it, in any case, an idea that Christians today must accept? I begin this concluding section with a consideration of these questions, but they will lead us to ask about how to interpret what the Bible says about the meaning of salvation and how God accomplishes it.

How Big Is the "Tent"? The Scope of Salvation

"I am the way, and the truth, and the life. No one comes to the Father except by me": so Jesus speaks in John 14:6. And in Acts 4:12, Peter declares that there is no name other than that of Jesus "given among mortals by which we must be saved." Both passages state that the only path to salvation is through Jesus Christ. In terms of the Bible's overarching story of God's redemption of the world, sin has separated humanity from God, and "there is no way back to God from the human side."[1] God, however, has now provided a way through Christ. The New Testament writers know about other religious paths, but these involve gods other than the God of Israel, whom they believe to be the only God. So it appears logical that Jesus, as the "way" to the Father, is the only way.

As Eugene Boring and Fred Craddock observe, however, John 14:6 does *not* state "that adherents of other religions are doomed if they do not make a personal profession of faith in Jesus before they die."[2] Neither this passage nor Acts 4:12 denies that God could grant salvation to persons *on the basis of* Jesus' life, death, and resurrection, whether or not they make such a profession. Neither passage mentions such a possibility, but other passages imply that salvation is available not only apart from confession of Christ but even apart from the "way" to God that Christ has opened. Matthew 25:31-46, for example, is a depiction of the last judgment in which the Son of Man grants eternal life, wholly apart from any expression of Christian faith, to those who perform deeds of mercy. And Acts 17:26-27 implies that persons in the Gentile world before Christ could have come to know God, for God has structured the world so that people could search for and perhaps find God. Similarly, in Romans 1:18-21, Paul's condemnation of the sin of Gentiles is based on the possibility that they could have known God through observation of the natural world.

Once again, we find competing perspectives within the Bible. And we again find that an aspect of our modern experience is helpful. In recent times, persons of different faiths have come to know each other in ways not easily available in earlier centuries, and we have learned a great deal about religions other than our own. It has thus become increasingly difficult for Christians to write off all other faiths as idolatrous or destructive or to believe that our Jewish, Buddhist, or Muslim friends—or even those who have no explicit religious faith at all—stand condemned in God's eyes. Many recent Christian theologians have therefore proposed doctrines of salvation that make room for persons who do not claim the name of Christ. Some argue that there are persons who know God in their hearts, without acknowledging God with their minds, in the same way that Christians know God through Christ. Others believe there are many paths to salvation, not all of which are parallel to the Christian path. Some think that all salvation is dependent upon Christ, while others think God offers salvation to those outside the Christian fold on a different basis. None of those I have in mind, however, deny that Christians experience salvation in Christ. And this is a point on which the New Testament has no ambiguity at all. When we ask precisely *how* God saves through Christ, however, the issue becomes more complex.

Reflecting on "Atonement"

The notion that the death of Jesus reunites sinful humanity with God is central to the New Testament. Church doctrine has understood this process of reunion through the concept of atonement—a word derived "from the combination 'at + one + ment' in Middle English, where it carried the sense of reconciliation."[3] The Bible uses various terms, drawn from different spheres of human experience, to express this reunion. In Mark 10:45, Jesus refers to his death as a "ransom," while in 2 Corinthians 5:18, Paul uses the term "reconciliation" to indicate that through Christ, God discounts human trespasses. John 1:29 alludes to the sacrificial cult in the Jerusalem temple, referring to Jesus as "the lamb of God who takes away the sin of the world." But when in Mark 14:24 Jesus refers to the cup of wine at the last supper as his "blood of the covenant," the imagery is drawn not from the temple cult but from the ceremonial ratification of the covenant between God and the people of Israel in Exodus 24:6-8.

Other New Testament passages present Jesus' death and resurrection as a triumph over the powers of evil and/or an act of liberation from sin and death. Colossians 2:15 proclaims that through Christ's death and resurrection, God "disarmed the rulers and authorities and made a public example of them, triumphing over them." The phrase "rulers and authorities" probably refers to both supernatural powers and their manifestation in oppressive earthly governments. Paul treads on similar ground in Galatians 1:4, where he refers to Jesus Christ as the one "who gave himself for our sins to set us free from the present evil age." This passage combines the motif of defeating the powers of evil with that of liberation. And we find the same combination in Revelation 1:5b-6: "To him who loves us and freed us from our sins by his blood . . . be glory and dominion forever and ever." In 1 Corinthians 15:12-28, Paul proclaims the resurrection as beginning a victorious process that culminates in the defeat not only of the powers of evil but of death itself, which he names "the last enemy" (15:26).

The New Testament thus offers various ways of speaking of Christ's death and resurrection as redemptive. What we do not find, however, is an explanation of *how* this event accomplishes the work of salvation—that is, how it atones for sin, defeats evil, establishes a (new) covenant, or liberates human beings. Therefore, theologians through the ages have proposed various atonement theories to fill the gap. This is entirely appropriate, but it is unfortunate that sometimes one of these theories has become enshrined as absolute truth and made into a test of one's faithfulness to the Bible.

Since medieval times, Western Christianity has been engaged in debates primarily between two major types of theories. On one end of the spectrum, we find the various satisfaction and substitution theories. The term *satisfaction* indicates that Christ's death was necessary to satisfy God's honor and sense of justice. The term *substitution* indicates that Christ's death "pays the price" for human sin or "suffers the punishment" human beings deserve. On the other end of the spectrum is the moral-influence theory, according to which Christ's death demonstrates the depths of God's love for humanity and softens the human heart, awakening a desire for repentance.

The satisfaction and substitution theories depend largely upon a particular reading of Romans 3:25, which states that God "put forward" Jesus Christ "as a sacrifice of atonement by his blood." However, the precise meaning of the key term *hilasterion*, which the New Revised Standard Version translates as "sacrifice of atonement," is uncertain. Those who favor the substitution/satisfaction view generally interpret it as "propitiation," a term that indicates the turning away of wrath. Another interpretive tradition understands it as "expiation," which indicates the wiping away of sin but without the connotation of turning away wrath. So, if one comes to the passage with the notions of substitution and satisfaction in mind, one can find them here. But the passage itself does not demand such a reading. Nor does 1 Corinthians 5:7, where Paul refers to Christ as "our paschal lamb," or indeed any other New Testament passage.

Many Christians have criticized the notion that a loving God would demand the shedding of blood as a condition of human salvation. Why could God not simply forgive sin? Furthermore, some think this approach tends to disconnect the atonement from ethics, since it emphasizes Jesus' death so much that his deeds and teachings seem to play little role in the actual process of salvation. Nevertheless, for many Christians, these theories have become entrenched as the litmus test for faithfulness to the New Testament.

With respect to the moral influence theory, there are no passages that specifically make the softening of the human heart in the face of Christ's suffering and death the agency through which forgiveness or reconciliation is won. However, Paul does characterize Christ's death on behalf of sin precisely as a demonstration of God's love in Romans 5:8: "But God proves his love for us in that while we still were sinners Christ died for us." And it is everywhere evident in the New Testament that Christ's death and resurrection are the basis for a call to repentance that entails a person's willingness to take up one's own cross (Mark 8:34). On the one hand, then, many theologians through the centuries have rejected the moral influence theory as unbiblical, but on the other it has found considerable support among those who believe it is consistent with the New Testament's emphasis upon God's freely granted love and forgiveness.

In sum, the New Testament neither explains the "how" of the atonement nor provides irrefutable support for either the substitution/satisfaction theory or the moral influence theory, although each of these has wielded considerable influence on Christian thought. We do find in the New Testament, however, the persistent notion that Christ's work involved defeat of the powers of evil. Thus, long before the development of the medieval theories, Christian thinkers conceived Christ's atoning work as a victory over sin and death, and this understanding is the dominant theory of the Eastern Orthodox churches. Some modern theologians have embraced versions of this approach to atonement under the rubric *Christus Victor* (Latin for Christ the Victor). Those who accept this view stress that, whereas the other theories tend to focus on Christ's death, the *Christus Victor* theory emphasizes his whole life, including his deeds and teaching as well as his death and resurrection. And it can be stated in such a way as to avoid the notion that God demands the shedding of blood as a condition of human forgiveness. One can, for example, understand Jesus' death as the consequence of his nonviolent confrontation of oppressive power structures and the resurrection as God's nonviolent way of defeating those powers.[4]

Unfortunately, some of the early statements of this theory made use of the notion of ransom in a way that many theologians through the centuries have found objectionable. The problem they have seen is that when we take the metaphor of ransom literally, a logical question arises: To whom was it paid? One early answer was that it was paid to the devil, who held humankind in bondage, but then God tricked the devil by raising Jesus from the dead. But this raises serious objections: How could the devil have had a claim upon human beings, and how could a sovereign God have been put in the position to owe the devil a ransom? Thus, many modern theologians who embrace the *Christus Victor* theory delete this aspect and speak rather of a release from bondage to the forces of oppression and injustice.

Doing without a Devil

The deletion of the devil-motif from the *Christus Victor* theory is in keeping with a modern tendency to understand the biblical language about the devil in a nonliteral way. The notion of a personal devil is actually a latecomer in biblical thought, appearing only during the period after the Babylonian exile. When the term Satan appears in earlier literature (Numbers 22:22; Job 1–3; Zechariah 3:1; 1 Chronicles 21:1), the reference is not to the devil but to a member of God's heavenly court who acts as an adversary or accuser. In the story of the Garden of Eden, the snake is simply a snake; only in later writings do interpreters come to view it as the devil.[5] Furthermore, for many Christians in our time, while the image of Satan may serve as a graphic way of symbolizing the reality of evil, belief in the existence of a personal devil makes little sense. Far from explaining the origin of moral evil, it simply pushes that question one step further back. If God created a good world, where did such an evil being come from? In late, noncanonical Jewish writings, Satan appears as a fallen angel.[6] But this leaves unanswered the question as to how evil entered into an angel's mind. If we instead elevate the devil to the status of God's "evil twin," so to speak, we violate the Bible's most fundamental theological premise: the affirmation of one God, creator of heaven and earth.

But how, then, do we account for moral evil in a world that God created as good? The answer lies, quite simply, in human free will. Our ability to choose the good comes at the price of our ability to choose what is not good. No further explanation is needed. But, of course, we human beings do choose evil and find ourselves in bondage to it. And this is the premise of the biblical story of God's redemption of the world and the background of the doctrine of atonement.

The Quality of the New Life in Christ

However we understand the atonement, the New Testament presents Jesus' life, death, and resurrection as liberating human beings from sin and death and effecting reconciliation with God. It thus witnesses to a new way of life. Paul can therefore describe those who are in Christ as manifesting a "new creation" (2 Cor 5:17). When we are freed from bondage to those things that separate us from one another and from God, we experience the *shalom* God wishes for all persons. We can receive life as a gift of God and experience true joy. The message of the New Testament is thus a message of radical grace—our unearned acceptance by an infinitely loving God. But it is also a statement of God's radical demand—the responsibility that God places upon those who receive the unearned grace. The nature of that demand is the subject of the final chapter of this book.

> The New Testament message is of radical grace and demand.

CHAPTER 7

Life in the Spirit

The Gospel of Grace and Demand

"Follow me," said Jesus. The man seemed willing but asked one thing: "Lord, first let me go and bury my father." Jesus' reply, however, was blunt: "Let the dead bury their own dead" (Luke 9:60). In ancient Jewish society, the burial of one's parents was a sacred obligation. In denying this request, Jesus dramatically pronounced that loyalty to God takes precedence over any other attachments. Neither family nor social group, neither ethnicity nor country should undermine the absolute claim of the gospel. The grace it offers is radical, abolishing the guilt of one's past and opening a new future. But equally radical is the demand it makes. And any impediment to meeting that demand becomes an object of idolatry and a violation of the first commandment—to worship God alone.

When Christians say that they worship God, however, that does not automatically protect them against idolatry. Attachments to particular understandings of God have caused much evil in the world. Wars of conquest, terrorism, persecution, torture, enslavement, discrimination— all have been practiced in the name of God. We must therefore refine our definition of idolatry: any belief or commitment we are unwilling to examine is potentially idolatrous and an impediment to the work of the Spirit.

Any belief we refuse to examine is potentially idolatrous.

In chapter 5, I suggested how an inadequate approach to biblical ethics leads to the abusive use of the Bible in relation to the status and role of women, divorce, and same-sex relations. In this chapter, I return to biblical ethics with a different agenda. One could get the impression from contemporary debates that the central moral issues in the Bible are those related to sex, but this is simply not the case. I hope now to get to the heart of biblical ethics by asking how the Bible's message of grace and demand speaks to us today, by challenging our idolatries and offering us the abundant life of God's new creation.

Looking for Life in All the ~~Wrong~~ *Right* Places

The Paradox of Finding Life

The gospel message is inherently paradoxical. We find the paradox in its most dramatic form in Mark 8:34-35: "If any want to become my followers, let them deny themselves and take up their cross and follow me. For those who want to save their life will lose it, and those who lose their life for my sake, and for the sake of the gospel, will save it." The point is that the narrow pursuit of self-fulfillment does not lead to true life. Only when we dedicate our lives to God do we discover our true identity and purpose. But this demand is also a word of grace, because it leads ultimately to self-fulfillment. The element of grace is even more apparent in Paul's version of the paradox in Romans 6:3-4: "Do you not know that all of us who have been baptized into Christ Jesus were baptized into his death? Therefore we have been buried with him by baptism into death, so that, just as Christ was raised from the dead by the glory of the Father, so we too might walk in newness of life." Paul's point is that through baptism, we die to sin and are empowered to live new lives. Thus, in verse 14, he assures his readers that "sin will have no dominion over" them because they are "not under law but under grace." In Galatians 5:25, he describes this new freedom as life in the Spirit: "If we live by the Spirit, let us also be guided by the Spirit."

One dimension of life in the Spirit is the development of inner character; another is right action. Both are present in Romans 12:1-2, where Paul urges his readers to "be transformed by the renewing of [their] minds" in order to discern God's will. Paul's ethic is thus a Spirit-driven ethic of discernment, and the love-principle is indispensable to the discernment process: "for the one who loves another has fulfilled the law" (Romans 13:8b).

Loving Others as Oneself

In Matthew's Sermon on the Mount, the Golden Rule in 7:12 summarizes the ethic of God's rule: "In everything do to others as you would have them do to you; for this is the law and the prophets." This injunction is an equivalent of the love command, as we can see in Matthew 22:34-40, where Jesus places love of neighbor together with love of God and proclaims, "On these two commandments hang all the law and the prophets." The so-called Golden Rule helps make the love command concrete, as does Matthew's description of the last judgment in 25:31-46, where the criterion for entering eternal life is whether one has performed deeds of mercy. To love is to treat other persons *as persons*, meeting their needs as we would like to have our own needs met. It also means recognizing the inherent worth of others and never treating them as means toward an end.

> To love is to treat others as worthy, never as a means to an end.

Concern for others, however, is especially difficult in a competitive society, in which people scramble madly to get ahead of one another. Jesus makes the task even harder by extending the love command to the enemy: "Love your enemies and pray for those who persecute you" (Matthew 5:44). Lest we think love of the enemy is merely internal, moreover, Matthew 5:39-41 interprets that love in terms of non-retaliation: "But I say to you, Do not resist an evildoer. But if anyone strikes you on the right cheek, turn the other also; and if anyone wants to sue you and take your coat, give your cloak as well; and if anyone forces you to go one mile, go also the second mile." Since the Greek words for "coat" and "cloak" refer to the inner and outer garments, we should hear these injunctions as hyperboles. To forfeit both these items would leave a person "not only penniless but naked."[1] But the force of these sayings is to undermine the self-defensive posture toward life that sets people against one another. Jesus demanded a commitment to a nonviolent lifestyle that forgoes any sort of revenge.

This might seem impossible, but that is so only if we sever the gospel's demand from its offer of grace. Jesus made his demands in the face of God's coming rule, and in his ministry he mediated the empowerment that came with that rule. In Paul's vocabulary the empowerment comes through the indwelling Spirit, but the basic idea is the same. What is impossible in human terms becomes possible with God's help, and what appears as impossible demand from one perspective is a liberating word from another. To "die" with Christ is, paradoxically, to be liberated from the rat race in which so many people are trapped. Those who find their true identity in Christ and their true worth in God's free acceptance of them no longer need to get ahead of others or to worship at the altars of success or popularity. To "die" with Christ is also to be liberated from the objects of idolatry that separate people from one another: social class, ethnicity, race, nationality, gender, sexual orientation. We do not find abundant life by associating with the "right" people, clawing our way to the top of the social heap or building group cohesion by excluding others. We find it through deeds of mercy toward and solidarity with "the least of these," whom Jesus identified as his sisters and brothers (Matthew 25:31-46).

We must be careful, however, about how we use metaphors such as losing one's life to find it. Although some people need liberation from self-inflation and a desire to dominate, others suffer from a deficient sense of self. The way of the cross is a way of humility, servanthood, and self-sacrifice, but true humility is different from groveling or self-deprecation. Loving one's neighbor as oneself presupposes love of self. Tragically, however, the church's call to servanthood often encourages a neurotic self-neglect that deprives people of their share of God's *shalom*.

And sometimes those whom society has assigned a subservient role accommodate themselves to the injustice by becoming loyal servants of unjust masters and courting their favor. What they need to give up is not the desire to dominate but their unhealthy need to please those who dominate them.

Carrying the cross of Christ does not preclude standing up for one's own human rights and dignity. It does preclude undermining the dignity of others. Indeed, it means joining the struggle of others to attain that dignity. Love of others thus involves more than acting kindly toward a circle of intimates. Paul's injunction to "work for the good of *all*, and especially for those of the household of faith" (Galatians 6:10; italics added) implies concern for the welfare of the whole human community. We see the same concern in his injunction to "abound in love for one another and for all" (1 Thessalonians 3:12). The love-based ethic of the New Testament is thus also an ethic of the common good.

Carrying Christ's cross includes standing up for human dignity.

One way to serve the common good is through the kinds of activities that churches and synagogues generally do very well—ministering to human needs through missional programs that address such problems as poverty, hunger, homelessness, domestic abuse, disease, and the suffering brought about by natural disasters. Ministries of this nature are essential to the church's life. There is, however, another arena of action on behalf of the common good that Christians have sometimes been more reluctant to enter: the world of public affairs.

The New Creation and the Common Good

Love of others drives us into the public sphere because assaults upon human welfare come not only from individuals but also from social and political systems. The indignities that African Americans suffered for so long in the south were not caused by individual prejudice alone. They were the products of a system of segregation enforced by social pressure, economic threat, state and local law, early federal court rulings, and the failure of the U.S. Congress and executive branch to address the issue. Thus, liberation came only when the unrest among the oppressed became a movement that engaged both social and political powers.

To challenge custom and law is to question the assumptions on which many people base their lives. It is to expose idolatries, which is a risky thing to do. Those who live in what the New Testament calls the "new creation," however, empowered by the Spirit, are willing to take the risk.

In this section, I will explore four areas in which the gospel disrupts customary ways of thinking. I begin with an issue that affects us all, regardless of social or economic standing.

The "Groaning" of Creation

"Indeed, it was very good." These words from Genesis 1:31, representing God's evaluation of the created order, express a central tenet of the biblical faith: the natural world is fundamentally good.

Psalm 19:1, for example, proclaims the grandeur of the cosmos as a means of God's self-revelation: "The heavens are telling the glory of God: and the firmament proclaims [God's] handiwork." John 1 identifies God's word as the agent of creation (v. 3) and affirms the goodness of the material world by declaring that "the Word became flesh, and lived among us" (v. 14). Similarly, Colossians 1:17 proclaims that "in [Christ] all things hold together." Christ appears as "the vital principle of creation,"[2] suggesting there is a divine element within the material world itself. The Bible thus not only treats the natural world as God's good creation but also hints that it participates in God's divine being.

Modern, Western culture tends, however, to understand nature as an object to be manipulated for human purposes. Ironically, we can trace this tendency partly to the Bible. In Genesis 1:28, God grants humankind dominion over all other creatures and the earth itself: "Be fruitful and multiply, and fill the earth and subdue it; and have dominion over the fish of the sea and over the birds of the air and over every living thing that moves upon the earth." In addition, when the Hebrew people began to worship one God, they rejected the nature-deities of other cultures. No longer viewing the sun, moon, or other aspects of nature as divine beings, they understood God as the transcendent *creator* of nature. The Bible thus retains only fragments of the notion that nature participates in the divine. The Scriptures maintained a reverence for nature, but this was lost in the course of Western history as the Industrial Revolution led to exploitative practices that have ravaged the earth.

Of course, the Western attitude toward nature has had positive consequences also. Advances in medicine and means of production have made life materially better for millions of persons. However, with this progress has come the destruction of innumerable species of life, the radical depletion of nonrenewable resources, massive pollution of water and the atmosphere, and the threat of catastrophic consequences from global warming. It is, in fact, increasingly clear that we have developed an unsustainable lifestyle. As populations have increased and developing nations have begun to struggle toward a standard of living comparable to that in the industrialized world, the strain on the ecosystem has brought us near the breaking point.

Our problems are not unsolvable, however. From a biblical perspective, there is reason for hope, for God's promise to redeem the world is central to the biblical story. Jesus' announcement of the rule of God and Paul's affirmation of the work of the Spirit proclaim that we are not alone in our struggle to save the earth. In fact, in Romans 8:18-25, Paul anticipates the restoration of nature to its state before the curse on the ground in Genesis 3:17-18. Imagining creation as "groaning in labor pains," he declares that it will be "set free from its bondage to decay and will obtain the freedom of the glory of the children of God."

Jesus and Paul tell us we are not alone in our struggle to save the earth.

Some Christians regard this promise as referring only to the unilateral act of God at the close of the age. For others, however, it is an invitation to cooperate in the process of restoration. Medieval Judaism taught the concept of *tikkun 'olam*, the "repair of the world." Modern Jews have adopted it as a call to social justice, and Christians should do the same. If we believe that the natural world is sacred, and if we have concern for all humankind, we should understand action to save the earth as essential to the church's mission today.

To this end, individual lifestyle changes are indispensable. It is important to recycle, use environmentally safe household products,

Action to save the earth is essential to the church's mission today.

and reduce our use of energy and consumption of goods. But individual action is not enough. Even the availability of recycling is a matter of public policy, and problems such as industrial pollution, toxic waste, and carbon emissions demand action on a collective level.

Ideological commitments, however, often stifle progress on these issues. Whenever serious changes in our lifestyles are proposed, the issue of economic feasibility arises. How would such changes affect the economy? Would reduced consumption put people out of work? Would our standard of living plummet? These are legitimate questions that reflect a concern for the common good. The barrier lies not in the questions but in our refusal to examine our presuppositions as we seek to answer them—that is, our unwillingness to go beyond our understanding of how the economy *does* work in order to think creatively about how it *could* work. I therefore want to offer some suggestions that I believe are grounded in biblical faith but are seldom taken seriously by the economic establishment.

I acknowledge that I possess no expertise in economics. My focus, however, is on the presuppositions on which modern economic theory is based, not its technical aspects. And I draw on the views of persons highly knowledgeable in the field. Most particularly, I am indebted to a book by a distinguished economist, Herman E. Daly, and a renowned Christian theologian, John B. Cobb Jr.: *For the Common Good: Redirecting the Economy toward Community, the Environment, and a Sustainable Future.*[3] Daly and Cobb are two among many recent thinkers who are challenging conventional wisdom on economics at its core, largely because of the ecological crisis. I plead with my readers not to try to place these schol-ars' ideas on the standard spectrum of options running from conserva-tive to liberal. They challenge the assumption that every economy must be located along this spectrum and warn, "Unless the reader relaxes this assumption, this book cannot be understood."[4]

Daly and Cobb are trying to construct a whole new way of think-ing about economics. They reject centralized, bureaucratic planning in favor of a bottom-up, decentralized approach to decision making, while recognizing the role of government in setting "fair conditions within which the market can operate." They endorse "private ownership of the means of production" but "favor the widest possible participation in that ownership, including worker ownership of factories, against its concentration in a few hands."[5] Also, their commitment to the common good entails a focus on persons-in-community rather than individuals-in-isolation.[6] And although they recognize that some issues must be addressed on national and even global levels, their overall vision is one of small-scale, relatively self-sufficient economies based on local resources serving local needs.[7] They recommend the resettlement of the rural United States and a move away from the unsustainable practices of agribusiness back to family farms practicing sustainable agriculture.[8]

Mainstream economists—including those at all points on the con-ventional spectrum—routinely assume that economic growth is good. This assumption may seem justified, since the growing global popu-lation requires increased production of goods, and economic growth can help alleviate poverty. However, growth also involves increased use of resources and further environmental degradation. Daly and Cobb recommend limiting the economy to a scale that is appropriate for our finite ecosystem. They also argue that the standard ways of evaluat-ing economic health are misleading. Economics is a self-contained sys-tem of thought that does not take account of factors that lie outside its boundaries and therefore treats them as "externalities," which play no role in economic analysis. An economy can therefore appear healthy even though the resources on which it depends are being depleted and the entire biosphere is disintegrating beneath it. As these authors comment, when issues such as "the capacity of the earth to support life" are "classed as externalities, it is time to restructure basic concepts" and find new ways of thinking about economic issues.[9]

Essential to the vision Daly and Cobb offer are the stabilization of the global population and decreased consumption by persons in industrialized nations.[10] Population control presents enormous challenges, but if the alternative is destruction of the planet, we must find ways of doing this without violating human rights. Decreasing consumption also is challenging, because of the threats of unemployment and lowered standard of living. But Daly and Cobb make credible suggestions for dealing with these issues. If the United States were to reverse the trend toward globalization of markets and reindustrialize the country along labor-intensive and eco-friendly lines, new opportunities for employment would appear. Reduction of working hours also would make more jobs available. It should also increase productivity, which would enhance the profitability of companies and help make up for the decrease in wages.[11] In any case, the globalization of markets and an oversupply of labor tend to keep wages low, whereas Daly and Cobb recommend a policy of full employment with government as the employer of last resort.[12]

We must still ask, however, whether decreased consumption means a lower standard of living. This raises the issue of human values. Many commentators on modern, industrialized society argue that our present pattern of consumption is unhealthy not only for the planet but also for ourselves—physically, mentally, and spiritually. A simpler lifestyle with shorter working hours would be less stressful, leaving more time to enjoy family life, develop interests that feed the mind and spirit, take part in community affairs, and engage in social service. And, in truth, we do not really need many of the things we have come to desire, largely under the influence of advertising. It may be difficult to convince our culture at large of this, but those who profess biblical faith should not be slaves to the ideology of acquisition. For we profess to live by a different standard: "Do not store up for yourselves treasures on earth, where moth and rust consume and where thieves break in and steal" (Matthew 6:19).

I realize that these suggestions may seem hopelessly naive to some readers. What seems naive to me, however, is the notion that we can continue our present pattern of consumption without creating a global disaster. Furthermore, God's power to bring about change and do what seems impossible in human terms is central to the biblical story. God leads the Hebrew people out of slavery, topples the Babylonian Empire to bring the people home from exile, and promises a rule in which peace and justice prevail and the natural world is restored. On what grounds, then, do persons who claim a biblical faith pronounce the hope for a better world naive?

A simpler lifestyle would be less stressful, feeding mind and spirit.

Community, Poverty, and Riches

The ideology of unlimited growth is destructive not only of the environment but also of human community. When companies, seeking ever-increasing profits, abandon locations to find cheaper labor, lower taxes, and lax environmental and safety regulations, the result is massive disruption of the social fabric. When large numbers of workers must move to other parts of the country to find work, their family lives are disrupted, and they are disconnected from the communities where they built personal relationships and participated in community life.

These problems, however, remain invisible within the framework of the self-contained economic theory. The major tools for measuring the health of an economy contribute to the invisibility of these and other issues. These tools are the Gross National Product (GNP), which represents the total value of the goods and services a country produces in a year, and the Gross Domestic Product (GDP), which is figured in a slightly different way. The problem, as Carol Johnston notes, is that the GNP "counts *all* market activity as a plus," and the same is true for the GDP. This means that "such costs as environmental clean-up and the burden of paying for larger police forces as societies unravel are actually counted as positive contributions!"[13] Nor do these indexes measure the distribution of the wealth created by economic activity. Thus, a nation's GNP and GDP can be rising while many of its people are falling into poverty. In fact, we in the United States are witnessing an increasing gap between the rich and the poor, but our indexes of measurement do not record this fact. On this point in particular, our current economic arrangements stand in marked contrast to biblical principles, for nothing is more central to biblical ethics than its demand for economic justice.

We saw in chapter 4 how the great Hebrew prophets announced God's judgment against the oppression of the poor. It is important now to note how economic justice fits within ancient Israel's self-understanding as a community in covenant with God. As Richard Horsley observes, early Israel made a radical break with the imperial economies of the ancient Near East, in which the people basically served the rulers. Those in power took much of the people's produce to maintain the military forces that engaged in conquests and kept the empires intact. They also used the people's labor to build monuments symbolizing their rule and employed religion as a means of sacralizing their regimes. The Israelites, however, withdrew from this system to form "an alternative society in which the people no longer bowed down and served the Forces of civilization, but served a transcendent Force of freedom, who insisted upon justice in relations with other people, not hard labor."[14]

The ancient world knew nothing of our modern tendency to think of religion, politics, and economics as separate spheres of existence. The laws of ancient Israel embraced both sacred and secular matters, without distinction. The people's responsibility toward God embraced their responsibilities toward their neighbors. We therefore find in the Torah a remarkable set of provisions protecting the welfare of all members of the community.

Torah protects the welfare of all in a community.

At the heart of ancient Israel's view of economics was its attitude toward the land, classically expressed in Leviticus 25:23-24: "The land shall not be sold in perpetuity, for the land is mine; with me you are but aliens and tenants. Throughout the land that you hold, you shall provide for the redemption of the land." This means that all human ownership is relative; the land is God's. As God's tenants, however, human beings have a limited claim upon it. God has in a sense leased the land to families, and each family is entitled to its ancestral holdings. Any sale of the land is therefore temporary. If a family is forced to sell because of economic failure, the family retains the right to buy back the land when its fortunes are reversed (Leviticus 25:25-27). Leviticus 25:9-10 also provides for a Jubilee Year (every fiftieth year) in which the families who have lost their land can return to their property. We are unsure whether this was actually practiced or remained an ideal. Either way, it reveals the intention, also expressed in the promise in Deuteronomy 15:4-5, that if the people obey God's commandments, "there will be no one in need" among them.

To achieve that goal, the Torah commanded lending to needy neighbors (Deuteronomy 15:7-11), coupled with a prohibition of interest taking (Exodus 22:25), and the cancellation of all debts every seven years (Deuteronomy 15:1-2). It also forbade farmers to harvest to the edges of their fields, granting both the Israelite poor and resident aliens (!) the right to glean what was left (Leviticus 19:9-10).

> Laws like the Jubilee Year intend that "there will be no one in need."

In withdrawing from the imperial economies, early Israel also rejected monarchical rule. There are two strains of tradition in the books of Samuel, one favoring the establishment of a royal household and another that interprets the desire for a king as a rejection of God. We therefore find in 1 Samuel 8:11-17 a speech by Samuel that warns the people how a king would treat them. These excerpts capture the essence of the speech: "[H]e will appoint for himself commanders of thousands . . . and some to plow his ground and to reap his harvest, and to make his implements of war and the equipment of his chariots. . . . He will take one-tenth of your grain and of your vineyards and give it to his officers and his courtiers. . . . He will take one-tenth of your flocks, and you shall be his slaves."

This description fits what actually happened when monarchical government was instituted. The harsh rule of Jerusalem kings led to the secession of the northern tribes, which split the Israelites into two nations. The pattern of exploitation was found in both, however, and in both cases, the ruling class used religion to legitimate its power. Thus, as Horsley observes, "The monarchy stood in opposition to the Mosaic Covenant, in which Israel declared exclusive loyalty to God as their king precisely as a way of avoiding falling back into bondage to a human king."[15] Whereas the Mosaic covenant made God's protection of the nation contingent upon the people's obedience to covenant law, the rulers in Judah promoted a new version of the covenant that declared God's *unconditional* support of the House of David in perpetuity (2 Samuel 7:4-17).

It was against this background of exploitation by kings and their officers that the great Hebrew prophets spoke their powerful condemnations of economic injustice. Jeremiah, inspired by his loyalty to the Mosaic covenant, condemned the Jerusalem temple itself. Naming it a "den of robbers," he indicted those who appealed to the Davidic covenant as an assurance of God's protection even as they committed gross abuses (Jeremiah 7:8-15).

The heavy tax burden that the monarchies placed on the peasants was increased when a series of empires imposed further taxes as they consumed the societies of the ancient Near East. During periods under Roman rule, the Israelites paid taxes to the Jerusalem temple, the Herodian royal household, and Rome itself. The Herods used taxes to fund elaborate building programs, and the Romans exploited the subjects of their empire to feed their troops and the population of Rome itself. The temple was the center not only of religious life but of the Judean economy, and the tithes and offerings it demanded added to the burden. Although the religious authorities had no means of enforcement, those unable to pay "faced social ostracism, shunning, and vilification by Temple authorities."[16] Estimates of the percentage of peasants' produce paid in the combined taxes range from 20 to 50 percent, "a significant and damaging amount for those living near subsistence levels."[17] Faced with financial failure, many people had to borrow from the aristocracy, which added to the latter's wealth as the situation of the poor became ever more desperate.

In light of these circumstances, it is probable that Jesus' demonstration in the temple (Mark 11:15-19) was at least partly a protest against the exploitative practices of the temple aristocracy. In any case, the Gospels present economic justice as a central motif in Jesus' preaching of God's rule. We see this particularly in the beatitudes in Luke and Matthew. Following a formula of blessings and curses familiar from covenantal contexts in the Hebrew Bible (Deuteronomy 28),[18] Luke's version (6:20-23) is followed by a series of woes (6:24-26). Blessings on the poor (destitute), the hungry, and those who mourn are paralleled by woes upon the rich, those who are full, and those who laugh. The passage is not only an expression of solidarity with the poor but also a condemnation of the exploitative system that makes some poor and others rich. The economic dimension is clear in Matthew's version (5:1-11) also.[19] The shift from "poor" to "poor in spirit" does not, as many commentators claim, represent a "spiritualization" of the concept. The "poor in spirit" are those whose spirits have been crushed by oppression. Nor are the "meek" those who are mild-tempered. They will "inherit the earth" (land) precisely because they are the dispossessed—those who have lost their ancestral holdings to the rich and powerful. And in verse 10, we should translate the Greek work *dikaiosyne* not as "righteousness" but as "justice." The point is that those who are persecuted because they seek justice for the downtrodden will receive God's rule along with the poor themselves.

At other points, Jesus criticizes the scribes as those who "devour widows' houses" (Mark 12:40), proclaims the difficulty the rich will have of entering God's rule (Mark 10:25-27), and lambastes the Pharisees for neglecting "justice, mercy, and faith" (Matthew 23:23). Two lines in the Lord's Prayer reveal the economic dimension of God's rule: "Give us this day our daily bread" is a request of people who live in daily fear of impoverishment, and the petition "Forgive us our debts as we have also forgiven our debtors" has a literal as well as a figurative meaning. Those who pray the prayer commit themselves to keep the covenantal responsibility to forgive the financial debts of those who cannot repay. Along similar lines, Jesus follows traditional covenantal guidelines when he urges his hearers to "lend, expecting nothing in return" (Luke 6:35).

Those who are persecuted for justice's sake receive God's rule.

The theme of economic justice continues in other parts of the New Testament. Acts twice describes the early Jerusalem church as having a communal economy (2:43-47; 4:32-37), and it was central to Paul's ministry to take up a collection in all his churches for that impoverished community (1 Corinthians 16:1-4; Galatians 2:10). As we have seen, the book of Revelation condemns Rome for its exploitative practices. And the letter of James echoes the Hebrew prophets in its indictment of the rich who oppress the poor: "Listen! The wages of the laborers who mowed your fields, which you kept back by fraud, cry out, and the cries of the harvesters have reached the ears of the Lord of hosts" (5:4).

This last passage in particular should resonate with anyone familiar with the financial collapse in the United States in 2008, brought on by the rapacious practices of major financial institutions. But do the people and the leaders of the industrialized nations have the will and the courage to ask hard questions about our economy? Current economic theory assumes that there are actual "laws" of economics, ignoring the fact that all economic arrangements are human constructs. It also assumes that human beings act almost entirely out of self-interest, stifling all attempts to think creatively about how a new economy, focused on justice and ecological responsibility, might be possible. To that extent, contemporary economic theory stands as a major example of idolatry. The Bible, in contrast, invites us to think and act differently.

The creation of a new economy will be an enormous task, and I realize that the suggestions I have made leave many questions unanswered. I cannot pursue these issues further in this limited context, but it seems necessary to round out the discussion with two further points.

The Bible invites us to think and act differently.

First, in light of the financial crisis of 2008, significant changes are needed in the oversight of Wall Street and the banking industry. For example, mega-banks, deemed "too big to be allowed to fail," have largely abandoned their responsibility for the common good. Having found ways of making profits that contribute nothing to the economy or the common good, they have largely abandoned the responsibility to make loans to individuals and small businesses that are essential to the welfare of many communities. We should therefore consider breaking up these banks into smaller entities, as Leslie Muray[20] and many others have suggested, and strengthening local and regional banks that actually serve their communities.

Second, I do not see how any person of biblical faith can remain satisfied with a system in which some people are left in poverty, with inadequate health care. Some economists propose a guaranteed annual income, while Daly and Cobb suggest a negative income tax.[21] And many believe that the only way to provide adequate health care for all is through a national system of health insurance. The inevitable question, of course, is how to pay for such proposals. But programs such as a guaranteed income or a negative income tax could replace many of the patchwork of bureaucratically managed aid programs that currently exist.[22] Furthermore, although national health insurance would increase federal spending, it could save costs to most individuals by eliminating the enormous bureaucratic tangles and other expenses involved in paying through insurance companies.[23] New revenue would be needed, but if we would reformulate our entire tax system along genuinely progressive lines, with those in the highest income brackets paying their fair share, no further burden would fall on people struggling to meet their own needs. In any case, we must also ask about the long-range costs, both financial and social, of *not* addressing these issues—for example, the cost of treating illnesses that could have been prevented and the cost of dealing with crime, addiction, and other social ills that result from poverty.

My concern, however, is less with specific remedies than with the criteria we use to evaluate them. I would hope that persons who take the Bible seriously would make their evaluations on the basis of biblical principles rather than a preconceived economic ideology. In our current arrangement, human beings are treated as cogs in a machine, servants of a system that has taken on the quality of an idolatrous religion. For many people throughout the world, this system resembles Pharaoh's Egypt more than the covenantal economy enshrined in the Torah and

The biblical vision is of an economy that serves people.

retrieved as an ideal in the New Testament. That biblical vision is of an economy that serves people—one that works not for the advantage of a favored few but for the common good and that enhances our humanity rather than diminishes it.

Engaging "the Rulers of this Age"

To say, in biblical terms, that we are empowered by the Spirit to work for the common good does not mean our task is easy. Although Paul declares that those in Christ manifest a "new creation," he envisions the faith community as living in an in-between time, when "the present evil age" (Galatians 1:4) overlaps with the age to come. Forces that he identifies variously as "the rulers" (of this age), "authorities," and "powers"[24] are still active in the world. Scholars once debated whether these terms refer to demonic forces or earthly institutions such as governments. But Walter Wink has shown that "*[t]hese powers are both heavenly and earthly, divine and human, spiritual and political, invisible and structural.*"[25] That is, earthly institutions are the tangible manifestations of cosmic forces.

The New Testament view of these powers is complex, because Paul also says God instituted governmental authorities (Romans 13:1-7); and the author of Colossians states that they were created through Christ (1:15-18). Also, Paul lists angels among the forces against which the faith community struggles (Romans 8:38-39). What are we to make of all this? Wink argues that "the powers" have a legitimate place in God's creation but become corrupt when they are ignorant of God's plan. And when human beings give them the unqualified allegiance that belongs only to God, the result is idolatry. Thus, in Wink's words, "Even the good, made absolute, becomes evil."[26]

Christians should therefore exercise discernment in their dealings with these powers. They should cooperate with them when they serve the common good but oppose them when they demand idolatrous loyalty and stand in opposition to God. Often, however, particular readings of two biblical passages discourage Christians from confronting "the powers that be."

The first of these passages is Roman 13:1-7, where Paul counsels his readers to "be subject to the governing authorities." Some Christians think this means they must obey the dictates of any government that might happen to rule over them. To "be subject," however, does not necessarily mean to "be obedient to." The nonviolent civil rights demonstrators of the 1950s and 1960s remained subject to the laws of the southern states even when they broke the segregation laws. They acknowledged governmental authority by submitting to arrest even as they engaged in civil disobedience. It is clear, moreover, that Paul's ultimate allegiance was to God alone, since he was willing to suffer frequent imprisonment for the sake of the gospel. Nor did he shrink from indicting "the rulers of this age" for the unjust crucifixion of Jesus or from proclaiming that they are "doomed to perish" (1 Corinthians 2:6-8). In Romans 13, Paul warned his readers against conflict with the Roman authorities, but he expected them, when faced with a choice between obeying God or human authorities, to obey God.

The second passage is a saying of Jesus. Asked whether it is lawful to pay taxes to Rome, he replied, "Give to the emperor the things that are the emperor's, and to God the things that are God's" (Mark 12:17; Matthew 22:21; Luke 20:25). This saying has been used to support the notion that God instituted two realms—the religious and the secular—and human beings owe obedience to both. It is also the root of an attitude expressed in a letter to a major newspaper that claimed that "Jesus was politically neutral." The intent of such a claim is to delegitimate Christian social action, but it is based on a misunderstanding of the passage. Jesus' statement is actually a clever way of making a "subversive" point without getting into trouble—a well-known tactic among subjugated peoples. All Jews knew that *everything* belongs to God, and the notion of separate political and religious spheres would have been unintelligible to Jesus' listeners. The coin Jesus asked to see, moreover, was a denarius, which depicted the emperor and claimed divine status for him. As William Herzog comments, it was "a piece of political propaganda that staked Rome's claim to rule the cosmos."[27] Jesus implies that the coin must be given back to the emperor "because it is blasphemous and idolatrous,"[28] not because the empire is worthy of loyalty. Jesus could not say this directly without being arrested, but his hearers would have understood the point: "Pay the tax if you have to, but withhold your loyalty."

Knowing when to cooperate with authorities and when to resist calls for discernment, and there are no simple guidelines for that process. Sometimes, however, the right choice is clear, even though many have found ways of distorting the biblical witness in order to avoid it. Some Christians in Nazi Germany joined the Confessing Church, which opposed the regime; others embraced German Christianity, which supported it. Some Christians have supported murderous, totalitarian regimes in Latin America that oppressed the poor. Others, however, notably Archbishop Oscar Romero of El Salvador and a number of Roman Catholic priests and nuns, were murdered because they opposed these governments and stood in solidarity with the poor. Some Christians joined or supported the civil rights movement, while others

We must discern when to cooperate with authorities and when to resist.

opposed or ignored it. Is there any doubt as to which of these groups were faithful to the biblical witness and which were not?

Our choices are seldom so dramatic, and "the powers" that we face are not always governments. Large corporations wield enormous power; many use that power in ways that undermine the common good. They also use their great wealth to influence governments, so that the public sector and the private sector become almost indistinguishable. Individual citizens are virtually powerless in the face of these institutions, but collective action—through local congregations, national church bodies, and various public-interest organizations—can sometimes wield influence. Congregations and individuals can have an immediate impact by supporting organizations that help build small, local industries in the developing nations, freeing the people there from exploitation by corporations that run the global economy. In any case, the Bible clearly demands of those who profess to worship God that they challenge "the powers that be" whenever they oppose God's vision of a just society.

Nonviolence, Peace, and the Sacredness of Life

If the New Testament authorizes resistance of "the powers," it also issues clear endorsements of nonviolence, as in Jesus' call for nonretaliation in Matthew 5:38-42. I must therefore emphasize that the resistance I call for is nonviolent in character. Consistent with the approach to the Bible I have recommended, however, I do not believe we must interpret such passages as demanding absolute pacifism. There are times when I believe circumstances justify the use of violence in just causes, such as genuine wars of liberation or defense. War in any form takes an enormous toll on both the human community and the environment, however, and Christians should be prepared to oppose any war that does not meet strict criteria as just, absolutely necessary, and a last resort.

Necessity should in fact be the primary criterion for any exercise of violence, and for that reason, I find capital punishment to be totally unjustifiable. It has never been shown to deter violent crime, and it seems hopelessly self-contradictory to try to uphold the value of life by taking life unnecessarily. From a Christian perspective, the provisions for capital punishment in the Hebrew Bible are irrelevant, since Jesus' saying on nonretaliation begins with a rejection of the "eye-for-an eye" provisions of the Torah (Exodus 21:23-24; Leviticus 24:19-20; Deuteronomy 19:21). I would also add that the value of life as a gift of God is precisely what stands behind the entire framework of biblical ethics.

Concluding Summary

Biblical ethics is not a catalog of rules but a call for Spirit-driven discernment. It is a prescription for the good life—the life of *shalom*—that God intends for all creation. As such, it is a call for solidarity among human beings and between the human species and the natural world. Its ideal is love of God and neighbor, and we are learning to include the nonhuman world in that latter concept. But it is not rightly understood as pure demand, for it is based upon grace, which precedes and grounds the demand. It is thus an expression of life in the Spirit—the abundant, empowered life of the new creation in Christ.

Epilogue

The Biblical Witness and the Word of God

Years ago, I heard a story about a man who attended a lecture by a great theologian. Perceiving that the theologian was not a proponent of biblical inerrancy, the man waved a Bible in his face and asked, "Do you believe that this book is the word of God?" The theologian gently took the Bible from the man's hand and replied, "If this book *grasps you*, but not if *you grasp* this book." This experience of being grasped by the biblical witnesses, having our hearts and minds revolutionized by them, is what I commend as the source of the Bible's true authority. When those of us who are Christians force the Bible into a mold of our own making, however—when we try to mine it for scientific information, insist on its historical accuracy in every detail, or apply all its culture-bound prescriptions in a literal way to the complexities of life in our time—we stifle what we believe is the living word of God that has the potential to speak through it. And we also undermine its potential to speak to persons who might be attracted to some aspects of its teaching but are understandably put off by interpretations that, quite frankly, make both the scriptures and those who adhere to them look foolish.

What, after all, do Christians mean by "the word of God"? In the Bible itself, God's word cannot be reduced to words on a page. It is a dynamic reality that encounters human beings. It comes through prophets as a power that can convict people of sin but also bring hope. In the Gospel of John, it is the personal agent through whom God creates the world and who takes on flesh in Jesus of Nazareth.

The Bible's authority lies in being grasped and revolutionized by it.

Is it proper to speak of the Bible as the word of God? I believe that from a Christian perspective it is truer to the biblical witness to say the Bible is the potential vehicle of God's word. That is to say a great deal, because for those of us who profess Christian faith it means that through the Bible, God's word can mediate God's presence to us and grant us abundant life. But this will happen only if it does indeed grasp us, that is, only as we let the Spirit, speaking through the biblical writings, make us into a new creation. To the extent we do in fact become that new creation, we will also find ourselves sent out as witnesses to and agents of the peace and justice of the coming rule of God.

But what, then, might the claim that God speaks such an enlivening word through the Bible mean to persons outside the Christian community? At a minimum, I think, it might simply move them to ask what it is about the Bible that has engaged so many people through the centuries and encouraged some to accept it as authoritative. It could serve, that is, as an invitation to take the biblical witness seriously as a perspective on life that is worth listening to—as reflection on life's meaning and purpose, on ethical responsibility, and on the values by which we live our individual and collective lives. It cannot do this, however—either for those outside the Christian fold or for Christians themselves—unless we all cease to read it in ways that obscure its most creative potential. For only when we get beyond abusive uses of the Bible and explore its deeper insights does it have the power truly to "grasp" us and change our lives.

Notes

Introduction

1. Edward Connery Lathem, ed., *The Poetry of Robert Frost: The Collected Poems, Complete and Unabridged* (New York: Henry Holt, 1969), 224–25.

Chapter 2

1. Lee Martin McDonald, "Canon of the New Testament," in *The New Interpreter's Dictionary of the Bible* (Nashville: Abingdon, 2006), 1:544.

Chapter 3

1. Gerhard von Rad, *Old Testament Theology*, trans. D. M. G. Stalker (New York: Harper & Bros., 1962), 1:13.

2. Bernhard W. Anderson, *Creation versus Chaos: The Reinterpretation of Mythical Symbolism in the Bible* (New York: Association, 1967), 41.

3. Walter Brueggemann, *Theology of the Old Testament: Testimony, Dispute, Advocacy* (Minneapolis: Fortress Press, 1997), 533.

4. Terence E. Fretheim, "The Book of Genesis: Introduction, Commentary, and Reflections," in *The New Interpreter's Bible* (Nashville: Abingdon, 1994), 1:337.

5. Francisco J. Ayala, *Darwin and Intelligent Design* (Minneapolis: Fortress Press, 2006), 91.

6. Kirk Wegter-McNelly, "Science, Religion, and the Origin of the World," *Focus* (Winter 2009/10): 23–24.

7. Ayala, *Darwin and Intelligent Design*, 29.

8. Ibid., 28–29.

9. Ibid., 39–40.

10. Ted Peters and Martinez Hewlett, *Evolution from Creation to New Creation: Conflict, Conversation, and Convergence* (Nashville: Abingdon, 2003), 43.

11. Ayala, *Darwin and Intelligent Design*, 40.

12. National Academy of Sciences, *Teaching about Evolution and the Nature of Science* (Washington, D.C.: National Academy Press, 1988), 58; quoted by Ayala, *Darwin and Intelligent Design*, 103.

13. John C. Whitcomb and Henry M. Morris, *The Genesis Flood* (Philadelphia: Presbyterian & Reformed Publishing, 1988), xxvi, quoted in Peters and Hewlett, *Evolution from Creation to New Creation*, 90.

14. Ibid.

15. Ayala, *Darwin and Intelligent Design*, 78.

16. Peters and Hewlett, *Evolution from Creation to New Creation*, 27.

17. Ibid., 28.

Chapter 4

1. Barbara Rossing, *The Rapture Exposed: The Message of Hope in the Book of Revelation* (New York: Basic, 2004), 19.

2. I draw largely on Rossing, *The Rapture Exposed*, ch. 2, for my description of rapture theology and dispensationalism.

3. Rossing, *The Rapture Exposed*, 176.

4. See Robert Jewett, *Jesus against the Rapture: Seven Unexpected Prophecies* (Philadelphia: Westminster, 1979), esp. 21–22.

5. Rossing, *The Rapture Exposed*, 19.

6. Ibid., 48.

7. See, for example, James H. Charlesworth, ed., *The Old Testament Pseudepigrapha: Apocalyptic Literature and Testaments* (New York: Doubleday, 1983).

8. M. Eugene Boring, *Revelation*, Interpretation: A Bible Commentary for Teaching and Preaching (Louisville: John Knox, 1989), 164.

9. Rossing, *The Rapture Exposed*, 118.

10. Boring, *Revelation*, 221.

Chapter 5

1. Alice L. Laffey, *An Introduction to the Old Testament: A Feminist Perspective* (Philadelphia: Fortress Press, 1988), 17; emphasis original.

2. Mary E. Shields, "Adultery," in *The New Interpreter's Dictionary of the Bible* (Nashville: Abingdon, 2006), 1:57.

3. Joanna Dewey, "The Gospel of Mark," in *Searching the Scriptures: A Feminist Commentary*, ed. Elisabeth Schüssler Fiorenza (New York: Crossroad, 1994), 470.

4. Carol Myers, "Women in the Old Testament," in *The New Interpreter's Dictionary of the Bible* (Nashville: Abingdon, 2009), 5:891.

5. Elisabeth Schüssler Fiorenza, *In Memory of Her: A Feminist Theological Reconstruction of Christian Origins* (New York: Crossroad, 1983), 147.

6. For a summary of evidence regarding the pseudonymous authorship of the Pastorals, Ephesians, and Colossians, see Russell Pregeant, *Encounter with the New Testament* (Minneapolis: Fortress Press, 2009), 279–80.

7. David W. O'Dell-Scott, "Let the Women Speak in Church: An Egalitarian Interpretation of 1 Cor 14:33b-36," *Theology Bulletin* 13, no. 3 (1983): 90–93.

8. Victor Paul Furnish, "The Bible and Homosexuality: Reading the Texts in Context," in *Homosexuality and the Church: Both Sides of the Debate*, ed. Jeffrey S. Siker (Louisville: Westminster John Knox, 1994), 32; emphasis original.

9. M. Eugene Boring, *Mark: A Commentary* (Louisville: Westminster John Knox, 2006), 288.

10. Victor Paul Furnish, *The Moral Teaching of Paul: Selected Issues*, 3rd ed. (Nashville: Abingdon, 2009), 59.

11. Ibid., 65–66; emphasis original.

12. Mary Douglas, *Purity and Danger: An Analysis of the Concept of Pollution and Taboo* (London: Routledge Classics, 2002), 55; Bernadette Brooten, *Love between Women: Early Christian Responses to Female Homoeroticism* (Chicago: University of Chicago Press, 1996), 234.

13. Brooten, *Love between Women*, 234.

14. Ibid., 235.

Chapter 6

1. M. Eugene Boring and Fred B. Craddock, *The People's New Testament Commentary* (Louisville: Westminster John Knox, 2004), 337.

2. Ibid.

3. Joel Green, "Atonement," in *The New Interpreter's Dictionary of the Bible* (Nashville: Abingdon, 2006), 1:344.

4. See, for example, Denny J. Weaver, *The Nonviolent Atonement* (Grand Rapids: Eerdmans, 2001).

5. T. J. Wray and Gregory Mobley, *The Birth of Satan: Tracing the Devil's Biblical Roots* (New York: Palgrave Macmillan, 2005), 68–70.

6. Ibid., 108–9.

Chapter 7

1. Robert C. Tannehill, *The Sword of His Mouth* (Minneapolis: Fortress Press; Missoula, Mont.: Scholars, 1975), 70.

2. H. Paul Santmire, *The Travail of Nature: The Ambiguous Ecological Promise of Christian Theology* (Minneapolis: Fortress Press, 1985), 205.

3. Boston: Beacon, 1989.

4. Daly and Cobb, *For the Common Good*, 10.

5. Ibid., 14.

6. Ibid., 159–75.

7. Ibid., 268–97.

8. Ibid., 274–82.

9. Ibid., 37.

10. Ibid., 240–51.

11. Ibid., 312.

12. Ibid., 234–35, 309–14.

13. Carol Johnston, "A Whiteheadian Perspective on Global Economics," *Handbook of Process Theology*, ed. Donna Bowman and Jay B. McDaniel (St. Louis: Chalice, 2006), 193.

14. Richard A. Horsley, *Covenant Economics: A Biblical Vision for Justice for All* (Louisville: Westminster John Knox, 2009), 15. I have drawn largely upon Horsley for my discussion of biblical economics in this section.

15. Horsley, *Covenant Economics*, 57.

16. William R. Herzog II, *Parables as Subversive Speech: Jesus as Pedagogue of the Oppressed* (Louisville: Westminster John Knox, 1994), 181.

17. Warren Carter, "Taxes, Taxation," in *The New Interpreter's Dictionary of the Bible* (Nashville: Abingdon, 2009), 5:479.

18. Horsley, *Covenant Economics*, 107.

19. Mark Allen Powell, *God with Us: A Pastoral Theology of Matthew's Gospel* (Minneapolis: Fortress Press, 1995), 119–40; Donald A. Hagner, *Word Biblical Commentary*, vol. 33, *Matthew 1–13* (Dallas: Word, 1993), 87–96; Russell Pregeant, *Knowing Truth, Doing Good: Engaging New Testament Ethics* (Minneapolis: Fortress Press, 2008), 129–33.

20. Leslie A. Muray, "An Ecological, Democratic Faith and the Current Economic Crisis" (paper presented to the conference "Trends in Whiteheadian Ecology: How to Solve the Global Systemic Crisis?" Cité Universitaire, University of Paris, March 2010).

21. Daly and Cobb, *For the Common Good*, 313, 315–18.

22. Ibid., 315–18.

23. See the Physicians for National Health Program website (www.pnhp.org).

24. 1 Corinthians 2:6-8; 15:25; Romans 8:38.

25. Walter Wink, *Naming the Powers: The Language of Power in the New Testament* (Philadelphia: Fortress Press, 1984), 11; emphasis original.

26. Ibid., 49.

27. William R. Herzog, *Prophet and Teacher: An Introduction to the Historical Jesus* (Louisville: Westminster John Knox, 2005), 185.

28. Ibid., 189.